RAILWAY HISTORY IN PICTURES:
IRELAND Volume 1

An artist's impression of a summer train on the Waterford & Tramore Railway at the turn of the century. The locomotive is a 2-2-2 well tank, No 2, delivered to the company in 1855 by Fairbairn of Manchester, rebuilt in 1865 and again in 1896-7.

The rake of carriages is not without interest: the first was built by Dawson of Dublin about 1853, the second is identical with Dawson's second class carriages for the Dublin & Kingstown line, Ireland's first public railway, and was therefore built to a design originating with a gauge of 4 ft 8½ in, the fourth is representative of many second class carriages of the 1850s, the fifth is ex-Waterford, Dungarvan & Lismore stock and the seventh an ex-Waterford & Central Ireland four wheeler.

RAILWAY HISTORY IN PICTURES

Ireland Volume I

ALAN McCUTCHEON
MA PhD FRGS

AUGUSTUS M. KELLEY PUBLISHERS

NEW YORK 1969

Published in the United States of America
by Augustus M. Kelley Publishers New York
Standard Book Number 678 055483
Library of Congress Catalog Card Number 71–77872

Printed in Great Britain by
E. Goodman & Son Limited Taunton

CONTENTS

INTRODUCTION

Irish railway history is a long and complex story, the telling of which in pictorial form proved quite a challenge, and even on a liberal canvas of some three hundred illustrations, presented in two volumes, it has been impossible to relate more than a fraction of this fascinating tale. The two books consist of a number of units or themes, each comprising a set of photographs, with informative captions, and a brief introduction: the subjects of these range from locomotive development to railway architecture and design, from tourist services to narrow-gauge railways, and in the major themes applicable to the whole duration of Irish railway history, a chronological division has been made into periods, each represented by a section in the book. In this way it is hoped the detailed history of Irish railways will be given some degree of balance and symmetry, more than if the illustrations were presented haphazardly, or in a strictly chronological sequence. While some attempt has been made to cover the principal aspects of the story, from the many thousands of photographs inspected the selection presented here is a purely personal one, as is the thematic arrangement of material.

The photographs themselves have come from a wide range of sources and while an early resolution that the final selection should be arrived at by balancing a list of items which ideally one would like to include with, on the one hand, availability and on the other pictorial quality, has been adhered to as far as possible, one of the author's most difficult tasks has been to make a final choice from the thousands available, a task which inevitably has meant the rejection of many items of outstanding interest.

It is hoped that the pages which follow will be at once informative and entertaining; of interest to the layman as illustrative of a phase in the social and economic development of the country and to the countless railway enthusiasts as a personal selection of pictures highlighting a story of absorbing interest.

THE COMING OF THE RAILWAYS

In the pre-railway era Ireland was relatively well served by a complex network of roads and canals, though travel was, of necessity, a slow and tedious affair, enlivened only by the threat of the numerous foot-pads to pack horse and stage coach alike and by the novel attractions of the recently introduced fly-boat services operated across the country, from Dublin to the Shannon, on the Grand and Royal Canals.

Unlike Great Britain, Ireland had neither great mineral deposits nor emergent areas of heavy industry for which cheap water transport provided an ideal means of inter-communication, and the high hopes of the canal companies were in the main founded on a basic misconception of the relative advantages and disadvantages of inland water transport.

So, too, with the railways there was no pre-existing continuum of horse traction on waggonways of wood or iron from which steam locomotion could develop. Rather, railways were introduced to the country by the pressure of commercial interests appreciative of the significance of the new means of transport and anxious to be early in the fields of commercial expansion and financial speculation which they could see in the immediate future.

Thus, the first railways in Ireland, from Dublin to Kingstown in the south, completed in 1834, and from Belfast to Lisburn in the north (1839) were built more as a reflection of the optimism with which the new means of travel was already being viewed in Great Britain and the confidence which such interests had in the success of an extension of the railways across the Irish Sea. The southern line at first handled passenger traffic only whereas the Ulster Railway was from the outset a line for both goods and passenger traffic.

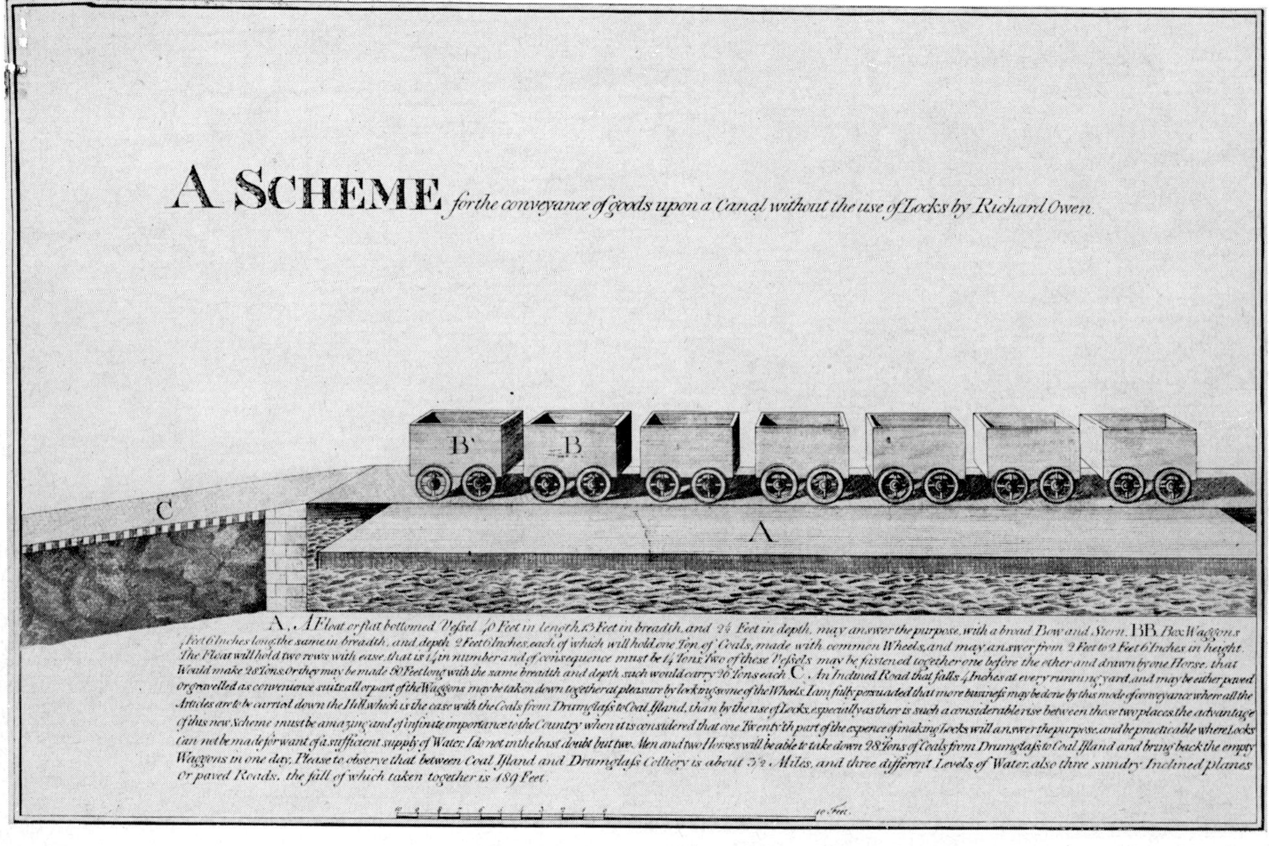

One of the few areas in Ireland where mineral traffic was of sufficient importance in the pre-railway era to prompt the construction of horse waggonways was near Coalisland in County Tyrone, where the need to provide ease of export for coal to Lough Neagh, Newry and Dublin led to the construction of a canal system in which short rail-roads were seen as one means by which gradients between water levels could be overcome. This illustration is of *A Scheme for the Conveyance of Coals upon a Canal without the Use of Locks, by Richard Owen.* This plan, by the engineer responsible for the greater part of the Lagan Navigation, was laid before the Irish Parliament in February 1787 and is one of a set of five drawings relating to the headward extension of the Coalisland Canal which were recently presented to the Public Record Office Northern Ireland by Mr R. S. Twigg of Cookstown, County Tyrone (PRONI, D.1701/2). Trains of box waggons were to be drawn from one level to the next and run in onto flat-bottomed floats moving up or down the several water levels extending from Coalisland up to the actual coal pits.

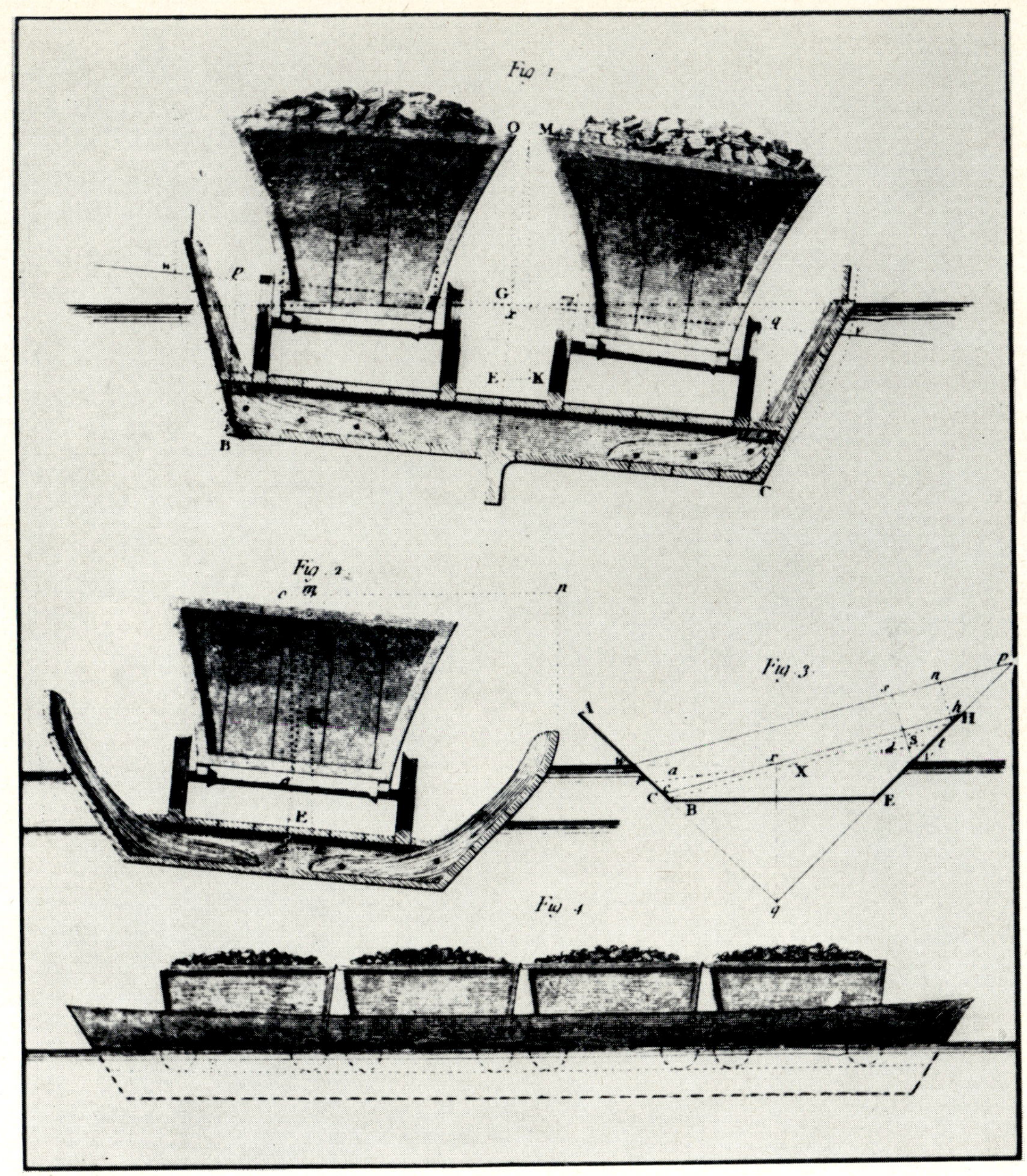

Coal trucks run in onto small 'tub-boats', on rails, similar to the type in use on part of the Coalisland navigation system, in east Tyrone, for the few years it handled commercial traffic, around 1780 (as illustrated in William Chapman's *Observations on Canal Navigation*, London, 1797).

General Observations

In making the Estimates I have supposed the line of Rails to be formed in the usual manner but I think it might be worthy of consideration if a different plan should not be adopted in Ireland where at least for the present as the transport of Merchandize and Manufactured goods cannot be expected to be large will almost entirely consist of Passengers and Agricultural produce the latter of which may in most cases be conveyd more advantageously by Horse Power than by Locomotive Engines for the advantageous use of these Engines that Loads should be taken at one time and at stated intervals, extensive Depots and Stores are also necessary; and to bring agricultural produce to them would in many cases be far too expensive and inconvenient to Farmers

At the terminus of the Lines, and also at the intermediate Towns these Depots would no doubt be useful and would be consequently erected. Corn merchants and others sending off large quantities of grain should no doubt have the means of transporting it by Means of Locomotive Engines from one terminus to another; but to make the Railway generally useful to the Country thro' which it will pass means should be given to the Farmers and Graziers along the Line to send their produce to the Different Depots or Market Towns either for the purpose of being consumed in those places, or to be stored in order to be afterwards sent along the Line in larger quantities by Locomotive power. To effect this object I would suggest that in the laying out main lines of Railway in Ireland. sufficient ground should be taken for four lines of Rail two for Locomotive and two for Horse Power; that the Embankment and Bridges should be constructed of the proper width for this purpose arrangement, but that in the first instance, only one line of Rails should be laid for Locomotive power and one Line for Horse power, these with proper

passing places would for years to come be quite sufficient. By this system the Farmers and others along the line might employ their own Horses at any moment they might find it convenient to send their produce to the Neighbouring Towns on the Line Manure, Lime and Building Materials could be taken back, and also many other articles which would be completely prohibited if a Locomotive Railway alone was established.

Such a system would also relieve the Locomotive Line, in a great measure from stoppages as the Country Passengers. and the Peasantry going to the Markets might be taken at a sufficiently rapid rate along the Horse Railway. and probably cheaper than by the Locomotive. The first cost of construction would be less, and an immediate return would be afforded. by the carriage of agricultural produce It will be necessary in the event of this arrangement being adopted to erect a Wall or Fence between the Locomotive Line and the Horse Line, but as Stone is plentiful in Ireland, and Masonry cheap. this would not amount to a very serious Sum. Probably it would be advantageous to place the Locomotive Lines in the Middle and the Horse Lines on the outside so that the Country Districts on each side of the Line would derive great advantage from it, their traffic would not interrupt the Locomotive Line by crossing it in the way it must if the Horse Railway was on one side only. There are several other Public advantages which I think this Plan would afford, such as lessening the annual expense of the County Cess and enabling small Farmers to send their produce to Market even by Manual Labour, instead of by Horses, which in a country where any thing that would give employment to the Labouring Classes would be of the greatest importance

Should the suggestion I have made as to forming Horse Lines on the sides of the great Lines of Locomotive Railways in Ireland be adopted, that portion of the Drogheda Longford Line which lies between Navan and Kells. and which is intended to be a Horse Railway. would not interfere with the great Locomotive Line proposed by the Commissioners. but on the contrary. would be so far a saving of expence; and both projects would tend to the mutual advantage and support of each other.

With the advent of commercial railways in Great Britain, it was natural that the British Government should regard the extension of rail transport to Ireland as desirable and a means by which the general condition of the country might be improved. A Royal Commission was appointed in 1836 to 'enquire into the manner in which railway communications can be most advantageously promoted in Ireland,' and after the most exhaustive investigations, during which the Constabulary was extensively employed in compiling a census of traffic, transport facilities and population, this 'Drummond Commission' recommended, *inter alia*, a railway system constructed on a 6 ft 2 in gauge and a main line from Dublin to Belfast following an inland route through Navan and Armagh. A remarkable atlas, the work of Henry Drury Harness RE, accompanied the Second Report of this commission, published in 1838, with maps of Ireland on a scale of 1 in to 10 miles, showing population, passenger traffic by public conveyances, and traffic volume as these existed in the country on the eve of the railway age.

The engineer who was charged with surveying and recommending the lines of railway in the north of the country was John Macneill, later to play such an important role in the development of the Irish railway network (see p 17 below). In May 1837 he addressed himself to the Railway Commissioners on the general role which he saw as likely to be played by the new means of travel and communication in a country not over-endowed with natural resources, and his proposals for combined horse and locomotive railways at the dawn of the age of steam locomotion in Ireland are of considerable historical interest. The pages reproduced opposite are from an ms notebook in the Public Record Office in Dublin (PWI/10/4, pp 28–31), entitled *Report of Surveys of Certain Lines of Railway Communication in Ireland executed under the commands of the Irish Railway Commission by John Macneill, C.E.* This was sent to the Commission with a covering letter dated 20 May 1837.

Already, however, the first locomotive railway in the country, from Dublin to Kingstown, had been opened. Some 6 miles in length and linking the capital with the port and watering place to the south, this line had been built to the English standard gauge—4 ft 8½ in—and had been opened to passenger traffic as early as 17 December 1834. The illustrations here are (top) a train leaving Westland Row Station and (below) passing along the sandy shore of Dublin Bay, over the embankment between Merrion and Blackrock, one of the features of the line.

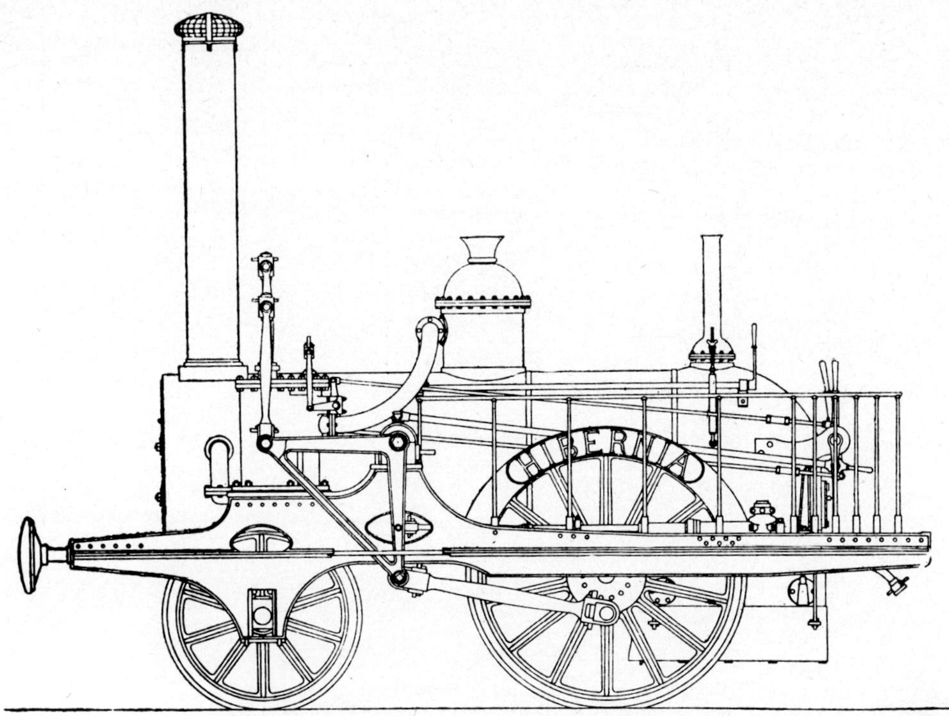

The locomotives of the Dublin & Kingstown Railway are of some interest. Of the six original engines for the railway, built in 1834, three were supplied by Sharp, Roberts & Co of Manchester and three by George Forrester of Liverpool, all with four wheels and tenders. These two groups are represented by **Hibernia** and **Vauxhall** respectively, the latter being the first steam locomotive to run in Ireland.   13

Sketch of Second Class Carriage on the Dublin and Kingstown Railway, with Patent Spiral Spring Buffer, as invented by T. F. Bergin, Esq.

Geometrical Section along the centre of Carriage, showing the application of Patent Spring Buffer.

A few years later, in 1839–40, the railway company began to build its own locomotives in Dublin, of which **Princess** was the first. These engines had the distinction of being not only the first locomotives built in Ireland, but also the first built by a British railway in its own works.

By the autumn of 1839 the stock of carriages on the Dublin & Kingstown Railway totalled fifty-seven, including first class, second class (both closed and open), and third class. The open seconds and thirds were roofed, and closed at each end. Shown here is a closed second class carriage, which a contemporary description considered

'superior to any at present in use on any railway in the United Kingdom. The elevation is more like that of a first class carriage. They are in three compartments, each calculated to hold eight persons. Besides the glass in each door, there are six square side-lights on each side of the carriage. These carriages are painted pale patent yellow . . . the framing of the carriages is all of Irish or Welsh ash and the sheeting, or linings, of mahogany . . .'

All the 'carriage-trucks' of the Dublin & Kingstown Railway were equipped with T. F. Bergin's 'patent spiral spring buffer . . .', Bergin being both engineer and secretary to the company.

14

ANNO SEXTO

GULIELMI IV. REGIS.

****

Cap. xxxiii.

An Act for making a Railway from the Town of
Belfast to the City of *Armagh* in the Province
of *Ulster* in *Ireland*.   [19th *May* 1836.]

WHEREAS the making a Railway, with proper Works and
Conveniences connected therewith, for the Carriage of
Passengers, Goods, and Merchandize, from *Belfast* to
Armagh in the Province of *Ulster* in *Ireland*, will prove of
great public Advantage, by opening an additional, cheap, certain,
and expeditious Communication between the Port of *Belfast* and
the City of *Armagh* aforesaid, and will at the same Time facilitate
the Means of Transit and Traffic for Passengers, Goods, and Merchandize between those Places and the adjacent Districts, and the several
intermediate Towns and Places : And whereas the several Persons
herein-after named are willing, at their own Costs and Charges, to
carry into execution the said Undertaking ; but the same cannot be
effected without the Authority of Parliament : May it therefore please
Your Majesty that it may be enacted ; and be it enacted by the King's
most Excellent Majesty, by and with the Advice and Consent of the
Lords Spiritual and Temporal, and Commons, in Parliament assem-
bled, and by the Authority of the same, That *Andrew Mulholland,*   Proprietors
John Kane, William Coates, John Charters, John Thomson, James God-   incorpo-
dard, John Curell, Hugh Wallace, George Greer, Hugh Montgomery,   rated.
James Macnamara, James Steen junior, *Robert Gunning, Lewis Reford,*
Henry Steen, John Gillis, John Dunvill, Edward Walkington, Robert
Gamble junior, *William Steen, Thomas M'Cammon, Sinclair K. Mul-*
holland, David Lindsay, Joseph Gillis, John Young, Randel Curell,
Daniel Curell, James Campbell, William Gray, John Read Allen,
[*Local.*]   11 M   *James*

The second railway in Ireland, and the first to cater for both goods and passenger traffic, was the Ulster
Railway, stretching south-westwards from Belfast along the Lagan valley. The Act of incorporation of the
Ulster Railway Co envisaged a railway between the Town of Belfast and the City of Armagh but the line
was built in stages, the first section, from Belfast to Lisburn, being opened in August 1839. The gauge
adopted here was 6 ft 2 in.

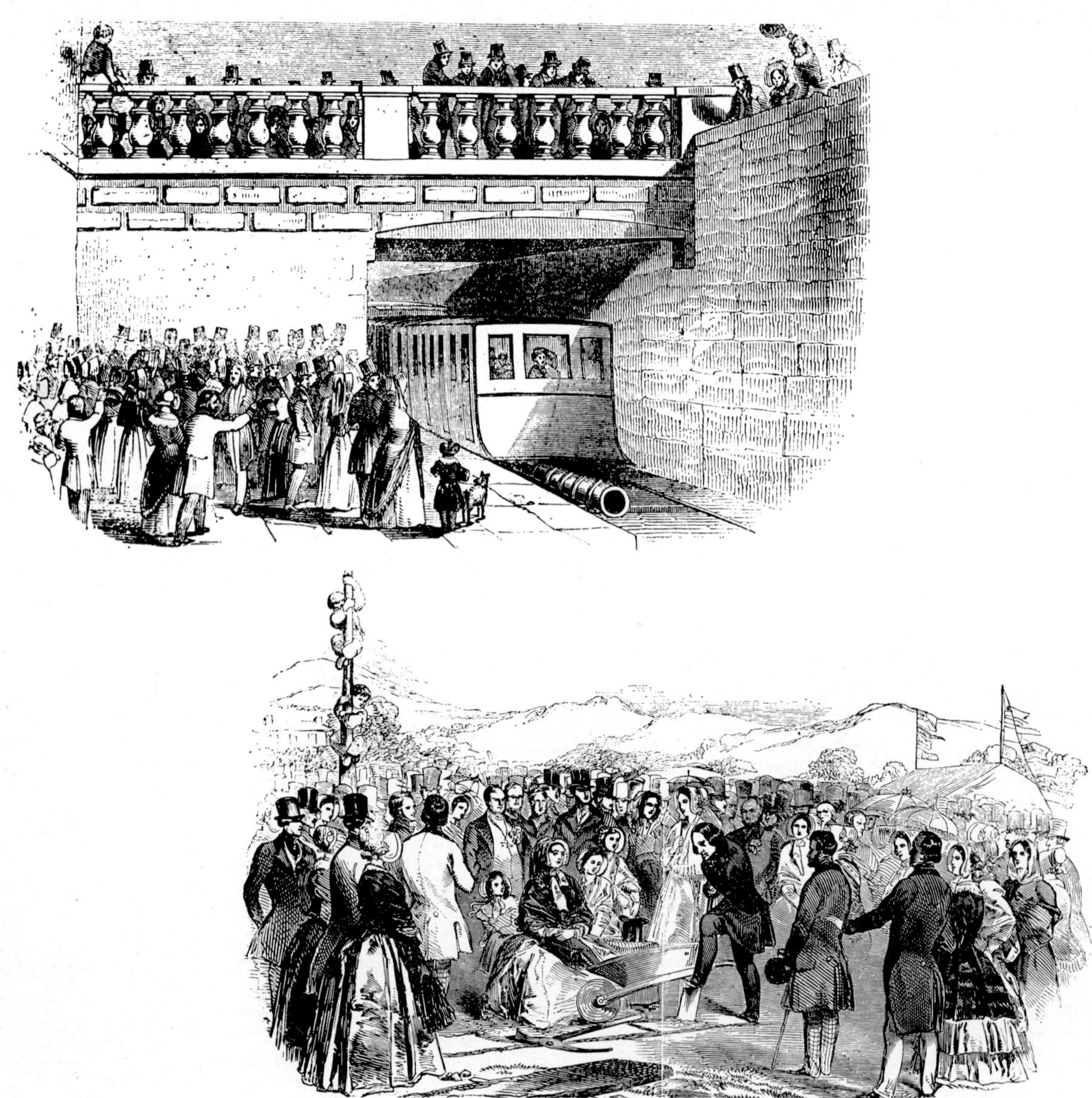

Meanwhile, in the south, the success of the Dublin-Kingstown line encouraged the Directors to extend their railway to Dalkey, '. . . on the atmospheric principle'. The $1\frac{3}{4}$ miles of atmospheric 'track' were opened on 29 March 1844 but despite optimistic anticipations from the numerous eminent scientists and engineers who visited the line it was neither a technical nor a commercial success and was converted to conventional steam traction by locomotive in 1855. The illustration shows the atmospheric line at Kingstown, with the train for Dalkey about to depart.

North and south, other railways quickly followed these early lines in the frantic years of railway mania. Up and down the country, first sods were turned in ceremonies attended by all the vigour and enthusiasm of the early Victorian era. Here we see the Earl of Bandon performing the opening ceremony on the Cork & Bandon Railway on 16 September 1845, with a mahogany wheelbarrow, suitably crested, and a spade '. . . of bright steel, the handle covered in red morocco leather, gilt lettered . . .' A labourer having previously loosened the turf, '. . . his Lordship took the spade and drove it into the yielding earth, amidst a mighty shout from the people . . .'

BELFAST & BALLYMENA RAILWAY.

HOURS OF DEPARTURE ON AND AFTER 1st JULY, 1848:

DOWN TRAINS FROM BELFAST, CARRICKFERGUS, AND RANDALSTOWN.

DEPARTURE FROM STATIONS.	No. 1. 1 2 3 Cl. Morn.	No. 2. 1 2 3 Cl. Morn.	No. 3. 1 2 3 Cl. Aftrn.	No. 4. 1 2 3 Cl. Aftrn.	No. 5. 1 2 3 Cl. Aftrn.	No. 6. 1 2 3 Cl.	Sundays No. 1. 1 2 3 Cl. Morn.	Sundays No. 2. 1 2 3 Cl. Aftrn.	1st Class. s. d.	2d Class. s. d.	3d Class. s. d.	Carriage 2 Wheels s. d.	Carriage 4 Wheels s. d.
Belfast,	8 0	10 30	12 15	4 15	6 35		9 0	4 0	... ...	... ...	... ...	... ...	... ...
Whitehouse,	8 10	... ...	12 25	4 25	6 45		9 10	4 10	0 6	0 3	0 2	... ...	... ...
Whiteabbey,	8 18	10 47	12 30	4 32	6 53		9 18	4 18	0 6	0 4	0 2	... ...	... ...
Carrickfergus Junction,	8 25	10 53	12 35	4 38	7 0		9 25	4 25	0 9	0 7	0 5	... ...	... ...
Trooper's-Lane,	8 28	10 56	12 40	4 41	7 3		9 28	4 28	0 10	0 8	0 5	... ...	... ...
Carrickfergus, Arrival,	8 30	10 58	12 45	4 43	7 5		9 30	4 30	1 0	0 9	0 6	3 6	7 0
Leave ditto for Ballymena,	8 12	10 40	... ...	4 25	6 47		9 12	4 12	... ...	... ...	... ...	... ...	... ...
Trooper's-Lane,	8 16	10 44	... ...	4 30	6 52		9 16	4 16	... ...	... ...	... ...	... ...	... ...
Carrickfergus Junction,	8 25	10 53	... ...	4 38	7 0		9 25	4 25	... ...	... ...	... ...	... ...	... ...
Ballynure Road,	8 35	... ...	... ...	... ...	7 10		9 35	4 35	1 0	0 9	0 6	... ...	... ...
Ballypallady,	8 43	11 10	... ...	4 55	7 18		9 43	4 43	1 4	1 0	0 8	... ...	... ...
Templepatrick,	8 50	... ...	... ...	... ...	7 27		9 50	4 50	1 8	1 4	0 10	... ...	... ...
Dunadry,	9 0	11 20	... ...	5 5	7 35		9 58	4 58	2 0	1 6	1 0	... ...	... ...
Antrim,	9 8	11 30	... ...	5 15	7 43		10 8	5 8	2 3	1 9	1 2	5 0	9 0
Drumsough Junction,	9 18	11 40	... ...	5 25	7 53		10 18	5 18	2 9	2 1	1 6	... ...	... ...
Randalstown, Arrival,	9 28	11 50	... ...	5 35	8 5		10 28	5 28	3 0	2 3	1 8	7 0	12 0
Ditto leave for Ballymena,	9 8	11 30	... ...	5 15	7 43		10 8	5 8	... ...	... ...	... ...	... ...	... ...
Andraid,	9 30	... ...	... ...	... ...	8 3		10 30	5 30	3 0	2 5	1 8	... ...	... ...
Ballymena, Arrival,	9 45	12 0	... ...	5 45	8 20		10 45	5 45	3 6	2 9	2 0	9 0	16 0

UP TRAINS FROM BALLYMENA, RANDALSTOWN, AND CARRICKFERGUS.

DEPARTURE FROM STATIONS.	No. 1. 1 2 3 Cl. Morn.	No. 2. 1 2 3 Cl. Morn.	No. 3. 1 2 3 Cl. Aftrn.	No. 4. 1 2 3 Cl. Aftrn.	No. 5. 1 2 3 Cl. Aftrn.	No. 6. 1 2 3 Cl.	Sundays No. 1. 1 2 3 Cl. Morn.	Sundays No. 2. 1 2 3 Cl. Aftrn.	1st Class. s. d.	2d Class. s. d.	3d Class. s. d.	Carriage 2 Wheels s. d.	Carriage 4 Wheels s. d.
Ballymena,	7 40	10 20	... ...	4 5	6 15		8 40	6 40	... ...	... ...	... ...	... ...	... ...
Andraid,	7 50	... ...	... ...	... ...	6 25		8 50	6 50	0 5	0 4	0 3	... ...	... ...
Drumsough Junction,	8 7	10 40	... ...	4 25	6 42		9 7	7 7	0 8	0 7	0 5	... ...	... ...
Randalstown, Arrival,	8 17	10 50	... ...	4 35	6 52		9 17	7 17	0 11	0 9	0 6	3 0	6 0
Leave ditto for Belfast,	7 53	10 28	... ...	4 13	6 30		8 55	6 55	... ...	... ...	... ...	... ...	... ...
Antrim,	8 17	10 50	... ...	4 35	6 52		9 17	7 17	1 1	0 11	0 7	4 0	7 6
Dunadry,	8 26	11 0	... ...	4 45	7 0		9 27	7 27	1 5	1 3	0 10	... ...	... ...
Templepatrick,	8 35	... ...	... ...	... ...	7 8		9 35	7 35	1 9	1 5	1 0	... ...	... ...
Ballypallady,	8 42	11 10	... ...	4 55	7 18		9 42	7 42	2 0	1 8	1 2	... ...	... ...
Ballynure Road,	8 50	... ...	... ...	... ...	7 26		9 50	7 50	2 4	1 10	1 4	... ...	... ...
Carrickfergus Junction,	9 0	11 27	... ...	5 12	7 35		10 0	8 0	2 8	2 2	1 7	... ...	... ...
Trooper's-Lane,	9 5	11 32	... ...	5 17	7 40		10 5	8 5	... ...	... ...	... ...	... ...	... ...
Carrickfergus, Arrival,	9 8	11 35	... ...	5 20	7 43		10 10	8 10	3 0	2 5	1 9	7 0	13 0
Leave ditto for Belfast,	8 47	11 14	3 0	5 0	7 22		9 47	7 47	... ...	... ...	... ...	... ...	... ...
Trooper's-Lane,	8 52	11 20	3 5	5 5	7 26		9 51	7 51	2 10	2 3	1 8	... ...	... ...
Carrickfergus Junction,	9 0	11 27	3 10	5 12	7 35		10 0	8 0	... ...	... ...	... ...	... ...	... ...
Whiteabbey,	9 10	11 36	3 15	5 20	7 45		10 10	8 10	3 0	2 5	1 8	... ...	... ...
Whitehouse,	9 15	11 40	3 20	5 25	7 50		10 15	8 15	3 4	2 7	1 10	... ...	... ...
Belfast, Arrival,	9 25	11 50	3 30	5 35	8 0		10 25	8 25	3 6	2 9	2 0	9 0	16 0

GENERAL NOTICES.

GRATUITIES.—No gratuity, under any circumstances, is permitted to be taken by any of the Company's servants.

The Company do not guarantee the arrival of the Trains at the respective Stations at the times stated, but will use their best endeavours to ensure punctuality.

LUGGAGE.—Luggage, to the following extent, may be taken, at the passengers' risk, free of charge :—first class, 112lbs. ; second class, 60lbs. ; third class, 40lbs. Excess Luggage at a moderate charge, according to distance.

Passengers are particularly requested to see their Luggage in and out of the Carriages.

The Company do not hold themselves responsible for any passenger's Luggage.

The door of the Booking Office will be closed, *punctually*, at the hours fixed for the departure of the Trains; after which no person can be admitted. The Clocks are regulated by Mr. Gray's Time-Keeper, Castle-Place.

PASSENGERS, to ensure being booked, should arrive at the Station FIVE MINUTES before the time fixed for the departure of Trains. All LUGGAGE to be FULLY DIRECTED.

CHILDREN under twelve years of age, half-fare ; and two Children under six, free, being members of the passenger's family.

Merchandise or other Goods will not be conveyed as Luggage, but will be charged for.

Carriages and Horses should be at the Station half-an-hour before the departure of the Train by which they are to be forwarded.

When Horses, Carriages or Cattle, are to be conveyed by the Train, notice in writing must be given the day previous.

Parcels will be forwarded by all the Trains. General Merchandise as soon as the Goods Stations are complete.

☞ ALL FORMER BILLS WITHDRAWN.

THOMAS H. HIGGIN,
GENERAL MANAGER.

FINLAY, PRINTER, BELFAST.

In the north, the stem of what was later to become an extensive system serving Counties Antrim and Londonderry was the Belfast & Ballymena Railway, opened in April 1848. This timetable of July 1848 contains several interesting asides in these early days of Irish railway working.

BELFAST & BALLYMENA RAILWAY.

QUEEN'S VISIT.

The **DIRECTORS** of the Belfast and Ballymena Railway beg to announce that they have made arrangements for the running of

Numerous Special Trains,

BETWEEN BELFAST AND CARRICKFERGUS,

So as to afford the Public an opportunity of witnessing that interesting sight, the Arrival and Anchorage of

THE ROYAL SQUADRON,

IN THE LOUGH OF BELFAST.

SPECIAL TRAINS from **BALLYMENA** and intermediate Stations will also be provided for the day on which **HER MAJESTY** pays her expected Visit to Belfast, with return Trains in the Evening. The Hours of Departure will be announced by Handbills, as soon as the days are known, and further information may be had on application at any of the Company's Stations. By Order,

Railway Office, 6th August, 1849.

THOS. H. HIGGIN, General Manager.

Little over a year after its opening, the Belfast & Ballymena Railway was providing special services run in connection with the royal visit of August 1849.

Some idea of the excitement and wonder with which the railway was greeted in the remote south and west of Ireland is conveyed by this wood-cut of March 1849 in which we see the arrival at Mallow on 17 March 1849 of the first train from Dublin, on what later became the GS & WR main line to Cork. It is recorded that

'. . . the train was welcomed with a tremendous cheer and waving of hats. On, on it came, the great engine panting, hissing, screeching and fuming, while the peasantry cheered or stood mute in wonder, occasionally uttering ejaculations of surprise and astonishment . . .'

The 145 mile journey from Dublin had taken $5\frac{1}{4}$ hours.

EARLY LOCOMOTIVES (PRE-1860)

A convenient watershed in early locomotive history on Irish railways is 1860, for design and practice occurring before then had little or no influence on subsequent development. Generally, passenger engines were 'singles', goods engines 'four-coupled', and the principal makers were Bury, Sharp, and Fairbairn in north Britain, and Grendon of Drogheda. The pre-1860 period did, however, include a number of engines of interest to the railway historian.

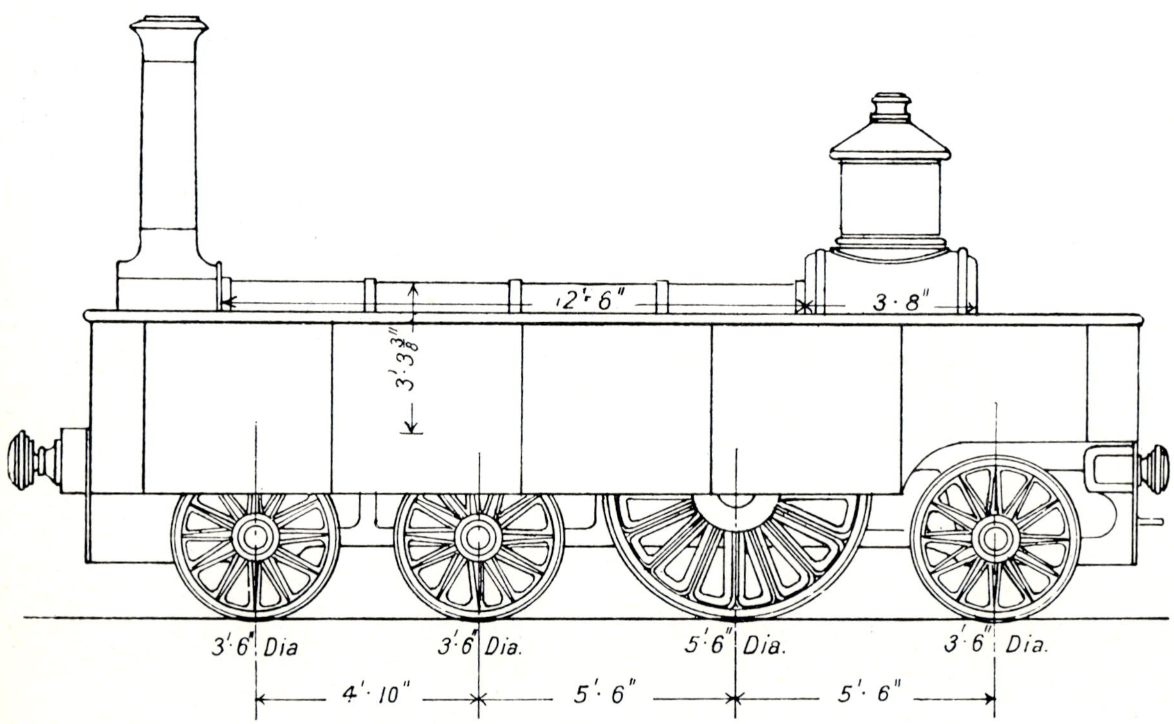

Tank engines for local traffic, of which there had only been a few early examples by Forrester on the Dublin & Kingstown and the London & Greenwich railways, again appeared in Ireland in 1846 when C. Tayleur & Co supplied three side tank locomotives of very unusual design (above) for the Waterford & Kilkenny Railway. The engines had very deep and long side-tanks and to distribute the weight, four axles were provided. The cylinders (14 in × 20 in) were inside and the third pair of wheels, 5 ft 6 in in diameter with T-iron spokes, were the drivers.

These were the earliest side-tank engines. The driver was apparently expected to oil the motion by getting underneath the engine.

Following the success of the small tank engines constructed on W. B. Adams' patent for the Londonderry & Enniskillen Railway, the Londonderry & Coleraine Railway directors decided to order six of these locomotives for the opening of their railway in 1852. All six were eventually built by Sharp Bros of Manchester. They were 2–2–0 well-tank engines with outside cylinders 11 in $\times$ 18 in, 5 ft driving wheels and 10 ft wheelbase.

A standard Sharp 'single', with 5 ft 6 in driving wheels, on a trial run on the Cork Blackrock & Passage Railway in May 1850. It is perhaps worth noting that this print shows a locomotive on loan from the Great Southern & Western Railway Co which by this time owned some twenty engines of this type and were persuaded to lend the Cork company two of them, pending the arrival of their own motive power.

An 0–4–2 goods engine, with tender, built for the GS & WR by Bury, Curtis & Kennedy of Liverpool and delivered as No 42 in September 1845. It continued in use until January 1880, when this photograph at Inchicore was probably taken.

An early locomotive of the Cork & Youghal Railway photographed at the Middleton shops, County Cork, sometime between 1866 and 1870, but delivered to the railway company by Neilson of Glasgow in 1860, the first engine in a second batch of three purchased in 1859–60. The locomotive, a 2–4–0 saddle tank, bears the number 63 of the Great Southern & Western Railway Company, which took over the Cork company in 1866, but the photograph cannot be later than 1870 when the engines were again renumbered. It is named after Lord Carlisle, the Lord Lieutenant, who paid an official visit to Middleton on 10 November 1859, gracing the railway with his patronage.

This 2–2–2 tank engine was built for the Dublin & Wicklow Railway Company by the Vulcan Foundry, Newton-le-Willows, in 1855. It was rebuilt in 1877 and in 1903 was sold to Robert McAlpine & Sons, contractors on the Waterford-Rosslare railway. This photograph was taken in 1903.

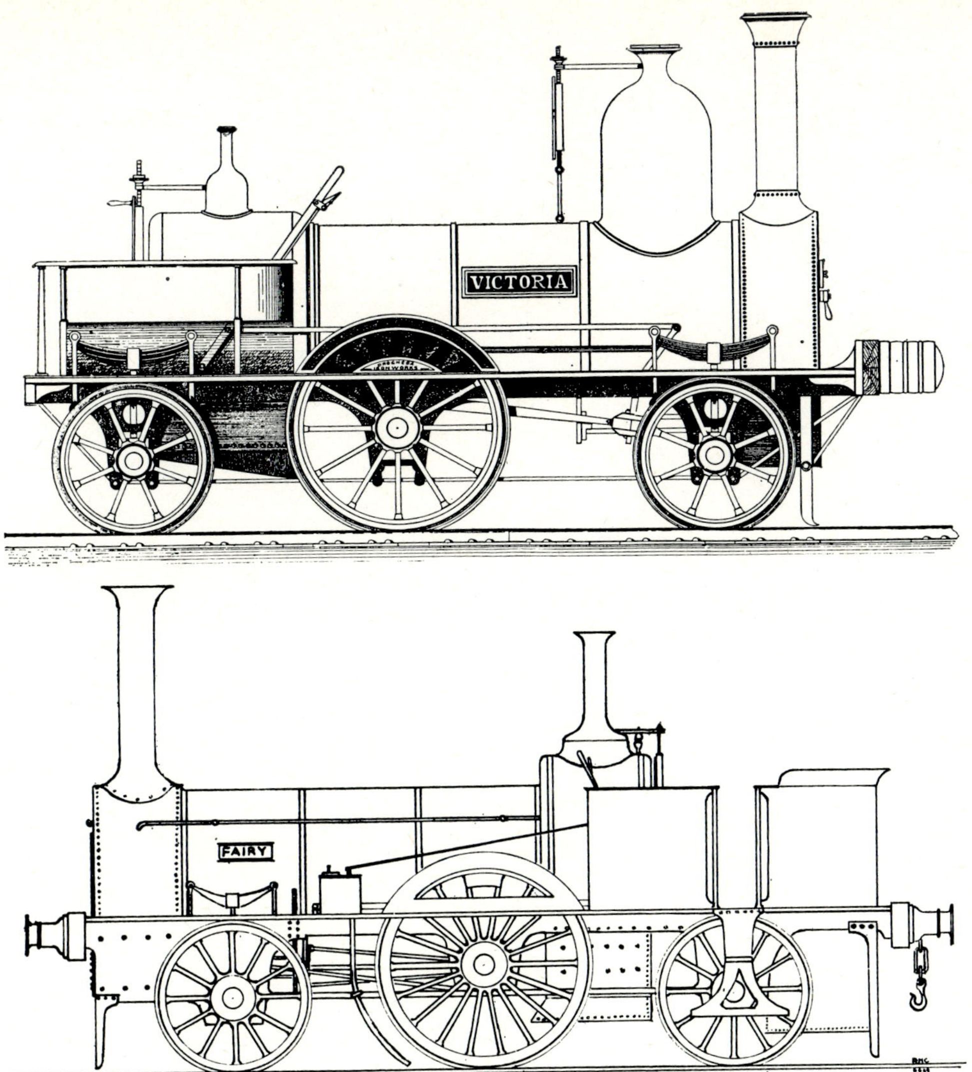

Victoria, probably the most famous locomotive built by Thomas Grendon & Co of Drogheda. This engine was built for the Newry & Warrenpoint Railway Company and began work on that line about July 1850 as a tank engine, having been purchased by William Dargan, who had leased the line which he had just constructed. It is perhaps worth noting that Dargan also entered into haulage contracts on the Dublin & Belfast Junction Railway, the Dundalk & Enniskillen Railway and the Waterford & Limerick Railway.

Victoria was withdrawn by the Newry Warrenpoint & Rostrevor Railway Company in 1885, at the time that company was being absorbed into the Great Northern Railway (Ireland). The locomotive was broken up in Dundalk shortly afterwards.

Midland Great Western locomotive No 27, **Fairy,** was one of three engines built by William Fairbairn & Sons in 1851 for working the 'Night Mails' from Dublin to Galway. They had cylinders 11 in × 15 in, driving wheels 5 ft, and carrying wheels 3 ft 6 in in diameter, and a weight of around $16\frac{3}{4}$ tons. In 1875–6 they were rebuilt, with saddle-tanks, and continued to work the Edenderry and Athboy branches until the 1890s. Four of these engines were ordered but only three delivered, the fourth being shipped to Brazil in 1852 and now preserved there, along with 9 miles of track, as a national monument.

RAILWAY ARCHITECTURE AND DESIGN
(PRE-1870)

The rapid expansion of railways throughout much of Ireland in the period 1840 to 1870, and the commercial and financial success which the major railway companies enjoyed at this time, resulted quite naturally in architectural and stylistic expression in railway structures, from station buildings of one sort or another, viaducts, tunnels and bridges, to detailed ornamental work in stone, iron and wood.

The capital accumulated by major undertakings such as the Great Southern & Western Railway Company, the Midland Great Western Railway Company, the Dublin & Drogheda Railway Company and the Ulster Railway Company, found expression in imposing, individually designed city termini, while here and there throughout the country, the skill of the early engineers and engineering contractors was tested to the full and is reflected even today in massive yet graceful monuments in stone and iron, functional to a degree yet strongly imbued with all the characteristics of the age in which they were created, when the horizons of rail transport seemed without limits and no physical obstacle was too great to halt the advance of the iron road.

The Dublin termini of (top) the former Dublin & Drogheda Railway Company (Amiens Street, 1844, William Deane Butler, Architect; now Connolly Station) and Great Southern & Western Railway Company (Kingsbridge, 1846, Sancton Wood, Architect; now Heuston Station).

A strong Egyptian influence, as seen elsewhere in Marshall's 'Temple Mill' at Leeds (1842) or in Macneill's 'Egyptian Arch' on the main Dublin-Belfast line (1851), is evident in the imposing facade of John Skipton Mulvany's Broadstone terminus of the Midland Great Western Railway, completed in 1850. The station closed in 1936.

The fourth principal Dublin station was Harcourt Street which until 1925 was the main line terminus of the Dublin & South Eastern Railway. Originally built for the Dublin & Wicklow Railway Company, it was opened in February 1859. The station building, designed by George Wilkinson, is a fine example of the blending of materials and textures, no less than of forms. There is a certain harmony between its rubble calp, brown brick and dressed granite and in a difficult and restricted site the planning has been ingenious and pleasing. The station closed on New Year's Day, 1959.

The remarkable castellated running shed at Inchicore, Dublin, built at the time of the construction of the main GS & WR line to Cork, in the late 1840s. This photograph was taken c 1875 and shows the 'up' road still laid with bridge rails (joint without fishplate apparent, left foreground). The somewhat primitive signal cabin was later replaced by a square box in a style closely similar to the main shed. Note also the two-armed signal of the period and the fluted cast-iron water column.

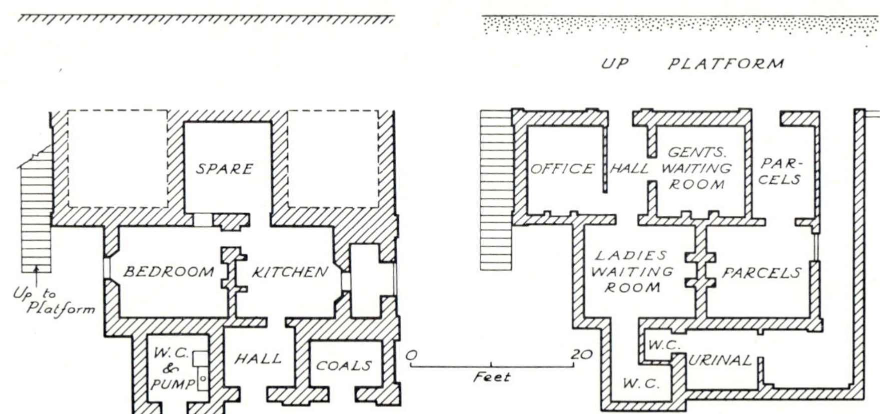

The oldest station building in the north of Ireland is the 'up' line block at Moira, between Lisburn and Lurgan, on the Ulster Railway extension from Lisburn to Portadown (Seagoe), constructed between 1839 and 1842. The station here, unlike the original buildings in Belfast (Dublin Road) and Lisburn which were later rebuilt, remains basically unaltered and is certainly not later than 1842. In the early days of railway working, and indeed up until the amalgamations which formed the GNR(I) in 1875–6, the station master's accommodation at Moira was in a basement, directly below the public accommodation at platform level. The station is now the direct responsibility of the Ministry of Finance in the Government of Northern Ireland and will be restored and used for administrative purposes.

Shown here is the station of 1842 with ground plans at platform and basement level.

In the construction of their line round Bray Head, the Dublin Wicklow & Wexford Railway Company had the advice of I.K. Brunel, and this reproduction of an early wood-cut of 1867, while primarily designed to illustrate a fatal accident which occurred there in August of that year, is of perhaps greater interest in that it shows details of bridge construction and permanent way characteristic of the great British engineer. Iron bridge rails were laid directly on longitudinal sleepers, with transoms to maintain the gauge. The viaduct itself was of massive timber beams fanning out from stone piers and resembled, on a small scale, the once familiar structures of the Great Western Railway in Devon and Cornwall.

As we shall see shortly, construction of the line from Dublin to Belfast involved several major feats of civil engineering. The other two main lines leading outwards from Dublin, to the south-west (Cork) and west (Galway), completed in 1849 and 1851 respectively, had also to negotiate difficult terrain. On the former, the viaducts at Mallow (opposite) and Monard (above), on the latter, the bow-string girder bridge across the Shannon at Athlone, bear testimony to the impetus already behind rail construction in Ireland. The principal contractor for all three structures was William Dargan, but the Athlone bridge was built by Fox, Henderson & Co. The viaduct at Mallow was blown up in 1922 and rebuilt with steel girders the following year.

Bagnalstown, County Carlow, an ornamental station in the baroque style built by the Irish South Eastern Railway Company in 1848.

Lisbellaw, County Fermanagh, a small country station on the former Irish North Western Railway Company's main line, from Dundalk by Clones and Enniskillen to Omagh, Strabane and Londonderry. The station here, built in the Gothic style so popular at that time (1858) in churches, schools and public buildings, had close parallels in other stations along the line, at Lisnaskea and Newtownbutler.

The station at Dundrum, County Dublin, opened on 10 July 1854, was to have been the terminus of the Dublin & Wicklow Railway and was constructed accordingly as an impressive single-storey mid-Victorian stucco block, with an open colonnade fronting onto the platform. Subsequent railway politics decreed that in fact Dundrum would be merely a passing, suburban station on the Harcourt Street-Bray line, though the station building, as originally conceived, was somewhat extravagant for this purpose.

The remarkable station building at Stranorlar, County Donegal, which was the terminus and administrative centre of the Finn Valley Railway Company, whose broad-gauge line from Strabane was constructed between 1861 and 1863. When the Finn Valley gauge was altered to 3 ft in 1894, Stranorlar became the main junction on the extensive narrow-gauge network of the Donegal Railway Company but the station there, which remained in use until the system closed down on New Year's Day, 1960, reflects the ill-founded confidence of an earlier era.

Helen's Bay, County Down (1864), on the Bangor branch of the former Belfast & County Down Railway system, was built by the chief engineer to the Belfast Holywood & Bangor Railway Company, Charles Lanyon, in close conjunction with the first Marquis of Dufferin and Ava of Clandeboye. The 'down' line buildings, with crow-stepped gables and pinnacled turrets, are clearly Scottish Baronial in inspiration, and from a private waiting room a glass-covered stone stairway leads down to what was formerly a courtyard, with stabling and carriage accommodation. From this, in turn, a fine ornamental archway, beneath the railway itself, opens onto a private driveway leading directly across the fields to Clandeboye.

On the former line of the GNR(I), linking Portadown with Londonderry by Dungannon, Omagh and Strabane, Dungannon was approached from the south-east up a gradient of 1 in 107 through a single bore tunnel half a mile in length. Construction of this was forced on the Portadown Dungannon & Omagh Junction Railway Company on their formation in 1857 due to the objections of Lord Northland who abhorred the idea of an iron monster belching smoke, sparks and flames charging through his demesne.

Two stations dating from 1863, Monaghan (top) and Gorey (Co Wexford), illustrate the different styles of the two companies concerned, the Ulster and the Dublin Wicklow & Wexford. Note particularly the signal cabin at Gorey, so characteristic of the Dublin & South Eastern system.

Charles Lanyon's over-bridge at Muckamore, County Antrim, built in 1847 for the Belfast & Ballymena Railway Company and still in use today.

The remarkable little station at Clonhugh, County Westmeath, on the Mullingar-Sligo section of the former MGWR, was originally built (1855) as a private station for the company chairman.

The Ulster Railway station at Portadown, County Armagh, constructed in 1861–2 to a design by Sir John Macneill. It is interesting to note that this building will shortly be demolished and replaced by a new station at Woodhouse Street on the west side of the Bann and nearer the town centre. This was precisely the site of the second Ulster Railway station at Portadown, opened in 1848, which Macneill's station replaced.

The fine sandstone bridges constructed on the first section of the Ulster Railway, from Belfast to Lisburn, between 1837 and 1839, are good examples of unhurried craftsmanship in masonry, implementing simple yet gracefully proportioned designs reminiscent of the canal and turnpike era and merging splendidly with the environment of the lower Lagan valley. Here we see (above) a small bridge spanning a private road at Lambeg, with (opposite) reproductions of two of the original drawings for Ulster Railway bridges (1835).

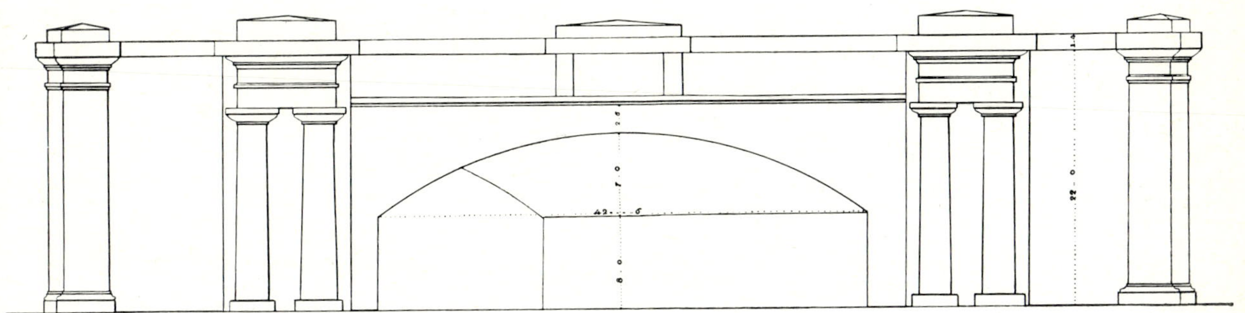

Elevation of proposed railway bridge over the Belfast–Lisburn turnpike at Derriaghy, County Antrim (1835).

Elevation of proposed turnpike road bridge over the Ulster Railway at Lisburn, County Antrim (1835).

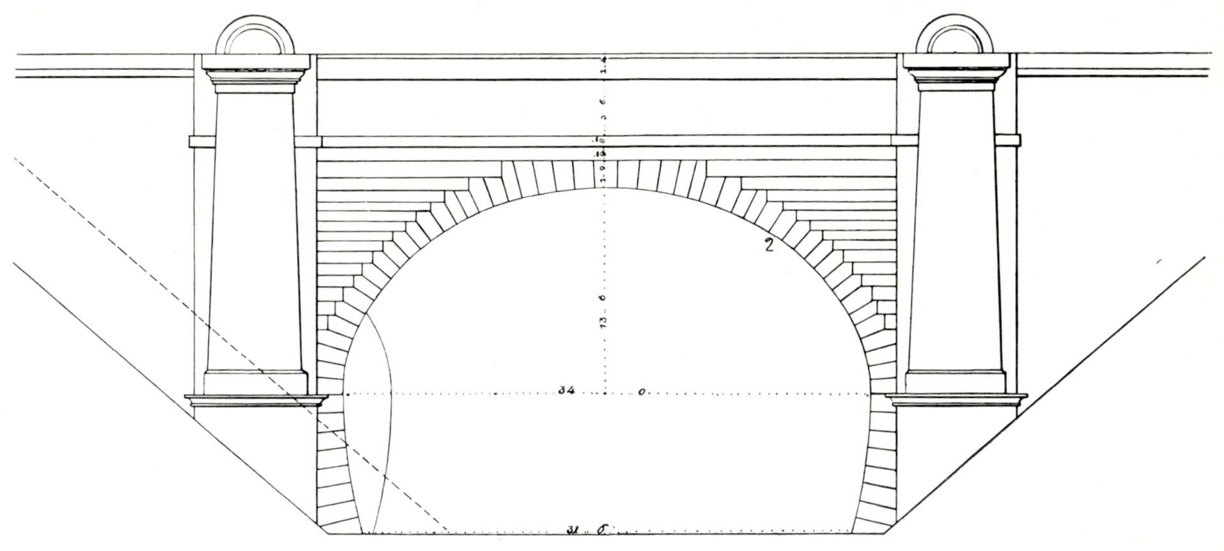

THE DUBLIN-BELFAST LINK

The Ulster Railway was extended from Lisburn by Moira to Lurgan and Portadown, reached in 1842. In 1844 the Dublin & Drogheda Railway Company completed its line northwards from the Amiens Street terminus. The Act incorporating the Ulster Railway had authorised construction of a line from Belfast to Armagh but no provision had been made for the linking of Portadown, on the Ulster Railway, with any southern rail head.

The link was eventually forged by the Dublin & Belfast Junction Railway Company and involved some of the heaviest engineering in the country, including the crossing of the Boyne by a lofty viaduct; the piercing of the mountains between Dundalk and Newry by deep cuttings in rough granite, and the construction of the gracefully curving viaduct near Bessbrook, County Armagh, by which the line is carried high over a tributary valley along the west flank of the Carlingford depression. The line was finally completed in April 1855, though through travel between Dublin and Belfast had been possible from May 1853, crossing the Boyne on a temporary wooden bridge.

Looking south from Baldoyle Bridge, on the Dublin & Drogheda Railway (1844).

The work of the Dublin & Belfast Junction Railway Company included several outstanding engineering achievements. At Drogheda the spanning of the Boyne valley was a major challenge. The original viaduct was constructed between 1851 and 1855. It consisted of a central lattice girder span of 226 ft, flanked by two shorter lengths, each of 141 ft, together with masonry approach viaducts to north and south. One of the chief difficulties experienced was in securing a sound footing for the four great masonry piers supporting the girders, the deepest foundation being set 43 ft below low water level.

The Craigmore viaduct carries the main line over a deep valley near Bessbrook, County Armagh. A gracefully curved structure of eighteen arches, each 60 ft in span and from 70 ft to 140 ft in height, the viaduct was built by William Dargan in 1851–2 to a design by Sir John Macneill.

Construction of large sections of the Dublin-Belfast railway was in the hands of a famous partnership in the history of civil engineering in Ireland. Sir John Macneill (above left) was consultant to many of the principal railway companies in Ireland at the time of maximum expansion. In his position as one of the engineers asked by the Irish Railway Commission of 1836 to submit a comprehensive schedule for the development of railways throughout the north and west of Ireland, and somewhat later as first Professor of Engineering at Trinity College, Dublin, his services were greatly in demand over the thirty years or so beginning in 1835.

William Dargan (above right), who as a young man acted as overseer under Thomas Telford in the construction of part of the Holyhead Road, including the embankment over the Stanley Sands between Holy Island and Angelsea, was by far the most important railway contractor in Ireland from 1833 until his death in 1867. A benefactor, philanthropist and far-sighted businessman, his lines included the Dublin & Kingstown Railway, part of the Ulster Railway, the Dalkey atmospheric line, the Thurles-Cork section of the main line from Dublin, the Mullingar-Galway section of the 'Midland', the Belfast & Ballymena Railway and the first sections of the Belfast & County Down system, part of the main Dublin-Belfast line between Dundalk and Portadown, and the line from Newry to Warrenpoint.

One of the most striking examples of architectural expression on Irish railways is Macneill's famous Egyptian Arch, constructed by Dargan for the Dublin & Belfast Junction Railway Company in 1851. It carries the main Belfast-Dublin line over the Newry-Camlough road about a quarter of a mile south of the Craigmore viaduct.

ULSTER RAILWAY.

THE PUBLIC are respectfully informed, that the First Section of this Line, from BELFAST to LIS-BURN, will be Opened, for the transit of PASSENGERS,

On MONDAY, the 12th of August.

HOURS OF STARTING :

From Belfast.	From Lisburn.
7, *A.M.*	8, *A.M.*
9, *do.*	10, *do.*
11, *do.*	12, *Noon.*
1, *P.M.*	2, *P.M.*
3, *do.*	4, *do.*
5, *do.*	6, *do.*
7, *do.*	8, *do.*

Each Train will stop at DUNMURRY, for One Minute, going and returning, to receive or set down Passengers.

Fares :

1st *Class Carriage,* 1s. *each Passenger.*
2nd *Do.* Do. 6d. *Do.*

No Reduction for the intermediate Stage.

Children......... *Half Price.*

JAMES GODDARD,
Chairman of Directors.

Belfast, 2d August, 1839. (587

The first section of railway to be opened which subsequently formed part of the main Belfast-Dublin line, was that part of the Ulster Railway from Belfast to Lisburn. Constructed between March 1837 and August 1839, the $7\frac{3}{4}$ miles of single track line, with a gauge of 6 ft 2 in, cost over £107,000. It is interesting to note that this line was built to the gauge recommended by the official Railway Commission summoned in 1836 to deliberate and recommend on the construction of Irish railways, but was subsequently relaid on the 5 ft 3 in gauge, as decreed by Act of 1846.

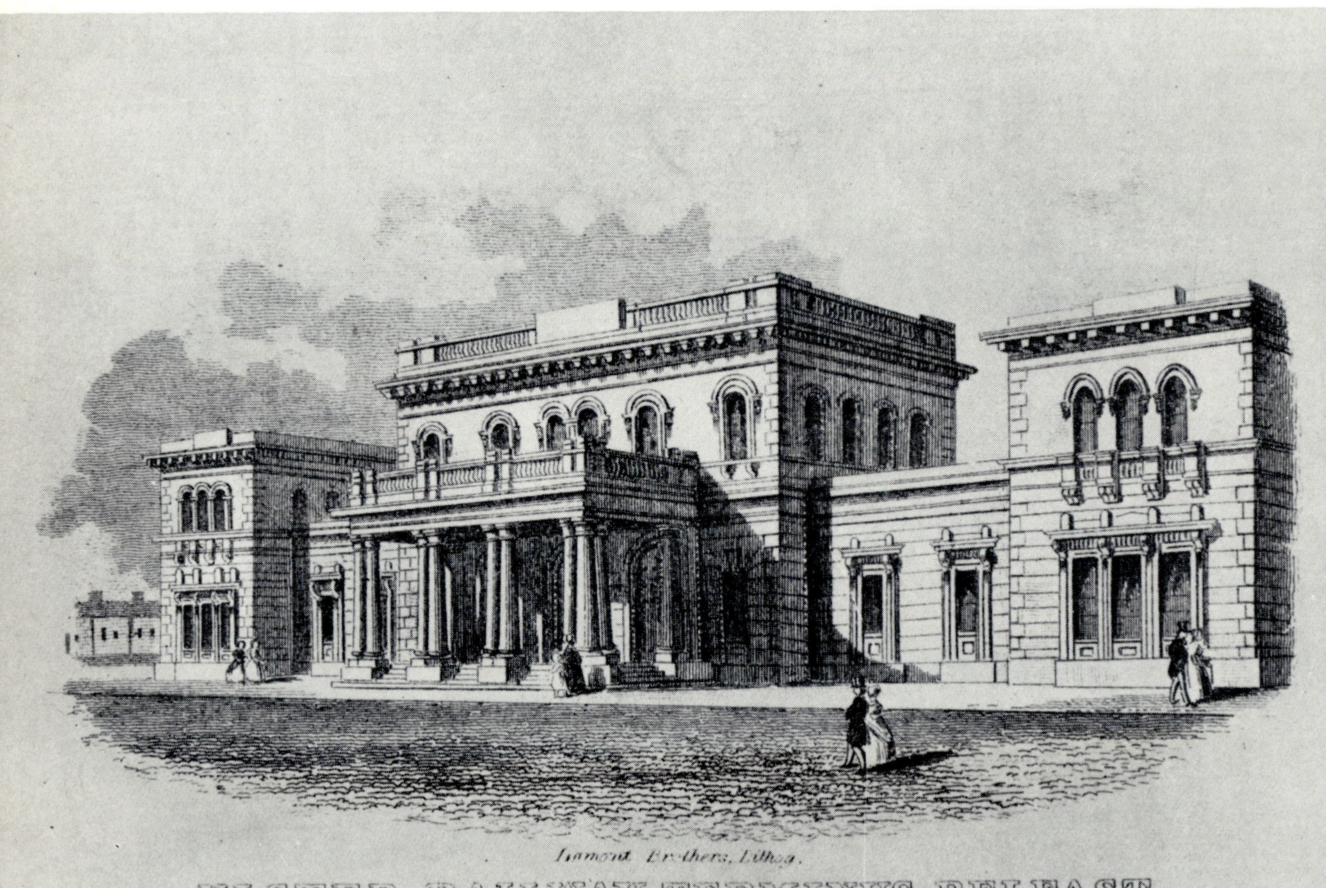

The new Ulster Railway terminus, Belfast, completed in 1848, replaced that which had served since the opening of the line to Lisburn in 1839. The building was demolished in 1969.

MINOR COMPANIES AND BRANCH LINE WORKINGS

One of the principal attractions of Irish railways was the degree of diversification existing within a relatively small area. Even with the amalgamations and subsequent standardisation of the last fifty years, the independent origin of many of the country's railways was until recently reflected in the general appearance of such things as locomotives and rolling stock, station buildings, railway fittings and furniture and even in the style and character of large and permanent features of civil engineering—bridges, viaducts and tunnels. Less tangible perhaps, but of no less significance, were the undercurrents of company pride and loyalty amongst the older generation of railwaymen; feelings lasting through the years, well into the modern era of enforced amalgamation and widespread closure. Both north and south, the majority of the overall mileage of Irish railways at the time of maximum extent, around 1914, had been constructed by small independent companies subsequently merging with larger, more powerful neighbours who in turn had been swallowed up by the national systems fanning outwards from Dublin and Belfast. This is scarcely the place to outline in detail the process of construction and amalgamation which was one of the most characteristic features of Irish railway growth. But, in that it left a legacy of minor railway systems independently conceived and constructed, and a much larger number of branch lines of more than passing interest, it has imbued the various by-ways of Irish railways with an appeal and interest far beyond their commercial importance.

Saddle tank No 3—**Dundalk**—of the Dundalk Newry & Greenore Railway, with a mixed train at Carlingford, June 1938. The Newry-Greenore line, occupying one of the most picturesque situations in Ireland, formed part of a system controlled throughout by the LNWR, whose interest stemmed from a desire to stimulate travel between Ireland and Great Britain through the new port of Greenore, County Louth. Locomotives and rolling stock were built at Crewe. The inset is the maker's plate on locomotive No 1, **Macrory,** of the Dundalk Newry & Greenore Railway Company.

An 0–6–4 tank, **Lough Melvin,** built by Beyer, Peacock & Co Ltd of Manchester hauls the regular afternoon goods from Enniskillen to the west, 17 July 1955. Two of these locomotives, built in 1949 but not introduced into service until 1951, were the last conventional steam engines built for an Irish railway company.

The Sligo Leitrim & Northern Counties Railway linked Enniskillen with Sligo through Belcoo and Manorhamilton. A line of great character, its promoters hoped that it would both stimulate iron and coal mining in County Leitrim and provide ease of export for the great cattle markets of the west. It opened in 1882 and closed in 1957.

The short 7 mile long Waterford & Tramore Railway, constructed in 1853, was throughout its entire existence quite isolated from any other railway system. It had until quite recently a tradition of remarkable continuity in locomotives and rolling stock. Seen here at Waterford is GSR No 483, originally Waterford & Tramore No 1, built by Fairbairn in 1855 and rebuilt in 1896 and 1924. When the train was photographed (July 1934) the engine was one of the last single-wheelers in regular traffic in Great Britain and Ireland. The line closed in December 1960. (See also frontispiece and Volume 2).

Characteristically headed by a 4–6–0 'Bandon tank', a passenger train crosses the Chetwynd viaduct at Ballinhassig, 4¾ miles south-west of Cork on the Cork Bandon & South Coast Railway. Constructed piecemeal between 1851 and 1892, this extensive system served much of west Cork. It closed in March 1961. The Chetwynd viaduct was 100 ft in height and the four 110 ft cast and wrought iron spans shown here are the originals by Fox, Henderson & Co (1851).

A rare view inside the Rocksavage shops at Albert Quay, Cork, taken in May 1953 and showing a 4–6–0 tank engine of the Cork Bandon & South Coast Railway.

On the Derry Central line at Garvagh: locomotive No 79, **Kenbaan Castle,** of the LMS (NCC) section of the Ulster Transport Authority, with the morning Magherafelt-Coleraine passenger train, 30 March 1950. Opened in February 1880, the independent Derry Central Railway, serving the towns and villages lying west of the Bann—Maghera, Upperlands, Kilrea, Garvagh and Aghadowey—was from the outset worked on lease by the Belfast & Northern Counties Railway Company, by whom it was purchased outright in 1901. The line finally closed in October 1959.

Another branch line of the York Road system left the main line at Cookstown Junction and served Randalstown, Toomebridge, Castledawson, Magherafelt, Moneymore and Cookstown, where contact was made with GNR(I). The Randalstown-Cookstown line was built between 1853 and 1860 and involved the crossing of the Main and Bann. Here an 'up' train crosses the viaduct at Randalstown in July 1938. The line closed on 1 October 1959.

48

The Timoleague & Courtmacsherry Railway was a short spur running from Ballinascarthy on the Clonakilty branch of the Cork Bandon & South Coast system. Completed in 1891 as a broad-gauge steam tramway, the section from Timoleague to Courtmacsherry ran along the seaward side of the public road on the southern shore of the Argadeen estuary. Here a 2–6–0 side tank, **Argadeen,** built by Hunslet of Leeds in 1894, prepares to leave the quayside at Courtmacsherry with two of the original bogie stock, which on account of the curves on the line were unusually short (30 ft). Note bell on locomotive for use on the road-side section.

One of the most picturesque of all Irish branch lines was that from Farranfore to Valentia Harbour, County Kerry. Completed in 1893 the line ran through wild, mountainous country, skirting the shore of Dingle Bay on narrow ledges high above the sea. The terminus at Valentia had the distinction of being the most westerly rail head in Europe. Here a mixed passenger and livestock train passes onto the viaduct at Cahirciveen in the early years of the century. Note the lime-washed waggons.

The Clifden branch of the Midland system was completed in 1895, from Galway through Oughterard, Maam Cross and Recess. The line skirted round the southern edge of the Connemara mountains and was built as a light railway on the broad-gauge, with financial assistance from the Irish Board of Public Works in Dublin. The railway company would have preferred a coastal route along the shore of Galway Bay but the Commissioners insisted on the adoption of the Oughterard route, which ran through very sparsely-populated country. Subsequently the Clifden and Achill branches came to play an important role in fostering the company's tourist traffic, with special services by road and rail from Westport, Mallaranny, Newport and Galway.

The illustration opposite shows navvies at work on the Clifden line in the early 1890s with, above, a general view of Clifden station shortly after the opening of the extension.

The Belfast & County Down Railway was a compact system extending throughout an area lying east and south-east of Belfast. The main line linked Belfast and Newcastle, with branches to Bangor, Donaghadee, Ballynahinch, Downpatrick, Ardglass and Castlewellan. The only part of the system remaining today is the short commuter line from Belfast to Bangor, along the south shore of Belfast Lough. The remainder of the company's network proved particularly vulnerable to competition from road traffic and closed as early as 1950.

The train shown above is on the 'down' main line at Dundonald on 5 July 1933, and consists of eight 'six-wheelers' hauled by locomotive No 26 (built Beyer Peacock 1892, rebuilt 1920), an 0–6–0 mixed goods and passenger engine which gave much good service on the Donaghadee branch line. The lower photograph is at Ballynahinch Junction on 3 January 1950, and shows the short branch line train (right), hauled by a 2–4–0 diesel electric locomotive built by Harland & Wolff in 1933, making connection with a main line train (Belfast-Newcastle). The diesel electric locomotive, 'D1' until 1937 and subsequently No 2, was introduced in an attempt to economise on branch line working. It went back to Harland & Wolff in January 1952 and has only recently been withdrawn from service.

An interesting Munster branch line was that of the Cork & Macroom Direct Railway Company, a 24 mile railway which commenced at a junction with the Cork-Bandon line about one mile from Cork and ran westwards through a fertile agricultural district by Ballincollig, Killumney, Kilcrea and Dooniskey to Macroom. The line was opened on 12 May 1866 and closed on 10 November 1953. The two illustrations here span the life of the railway, the upper item being a contemporary woodcut showing the arrival of the first train at Macroom, the other a photograph taken at Macroom on the last day of normal working. A 4–4–2T, CIE No 269, originally with the Waterford & Limerick Railway, is seen making up the last train prior to departure for Cork. Passenger services were withdrawn on this line as early as 29 June 1935.

The extensive system operated by the GNR(I) included a number of interesting branch lines, of which four are illustrated on this and succeeding pages.

Above we see a train from the Bundoran branch leaving Bundoran Junction for Enniskillen, headed by locomotive No 43 (GN class 'PP'), built at Dundalk in 1911, with the first two passenger coaches ex LNWR stock bought from the LMS immediately after the Second World War. The triangular junction here, with lines to Omagh, Enniskillen and Bundoran, was the point at which the famous 'Bundoran Express' from Dublin, its coaches crowded with pilgrims bound for Pettigo and Lough Derg, swung away westwards along the northern shore of Lower Lough Erne towards Ballyshannon and Bundoran, having followed the line of the 'Irish North' from Dundalk.

Here trains of rival companies are shown passing at Castlewellan, County Down, where the GNR(I) and the BCDR came in contact. The BCDR main line had reached Newcastle from Belfast in March 1869; not until 1880 did the GNR line from Lisburn reach Ballyroney, from whence the company was anxious to extend its line to Castlewellan and Newcastle. The BCDR was determined to prevent this and proposed an offshoot from their main line to the new rail head at Ballyroney. The problem was eventually solved by arbitration and as neither company would accept the other's proposals, a compromise was decided upon. Each company was to construct part of the intervening section, the GN from Ballyroney to Castlewellan, the BCDR from Newcastle to Castlewellan. Running powers were given to the former as far as Newcastle, to the latter as far as Ballyroney. The through connection was established in November, 1906. Shown here is GNR locomotive No 197, **Lough Neagh** (a 'U' class 4–4–0 built by Beyer Peacock in 1915) on the 'up' line, passing a passenger train headed by a standard BCDR 4–4–2 tank in June 1949, by which time the railway services of the Ulster Transport Authority and the GNR(I) were running without thought of past disagreements.

An interesting branch of the extensive 'Great Northern' system was the ill-fated Castleblayney Keady & Armagh Railway, begun in 1903 by a company glorying under that title but completed by the GNR between 1908 and 1910 to ensure that the Midland Great Western Railway Company did not extend its sphere of influence into Great Northern territory. The Castleblayney-Keady section closed as early as 1923. Here, at Irish Street Halt, on the outskirts of Armagh, GNR locomotive No 1, a 4–4–0T of the 'BT' class and the first engine built in the new shops at Dundalk (June 1887), operates a 'push-pull' service on the Keady line.

At many points on the Great Northern system there was insufficient traffic to justify construction of even platform accommodation, yet to provide a personal service the railway company made arrangements for trains to stop on request. Here a local train stops at Retreat Halt, near Armagh, in the summer of 1956, shortly before services were withdrawn.

An early view of the Bangor station of the Belfast & County Down Railway, taken around 1900 and showing the Belfast train, headed by a 2–4–0 saddle tank acquired from the former Belfast Holywood & Bangor Railway Company in 1884, about to leave the 'up' platform—the only one in existence at that time.

A passenger train at Athboy, County Meath, the terminus of the branch line from Kilmessan on the MGWR, the photograph taken early in the present century. The locomotive is one of the small 0–6–0 tanks designed by Martin Atock and introduced on the Midland in 1891.

LOCOMOTIVE DEVELOPMENT 1860-1900

The period 1860–1900 saw the introduction of locomotive types which were to last, basically unaltered, until the 1920s, or even later. The general lines of locomotive design laid down in this period were little altered half a century later, and it is a reasonable generalisation to regard the period as one of continuous development leading up to the hey-day of steam locomotion, early in this century. Passenger engines were now usually 'four-coupled', goods engines 'six-coupled' and while Bury, Fairbairn, and Grendon were no longer building, the Gorton Foundry of Beyer, Peacock & Co Ltd in Manchester came to replace Sharp Stewart as the main supplier of steam locomotives for Irish railways.

Considering the 1860 watershed in greater detail we note the following changes occurring in the various companies around that date: on the GS & WR the appointment of Alexander McDonnell in 1864 saw the introduction of the standard Inchicore types; on the MGWR the years 1860 and 1861 saw Cabry's standard designs replacing the older types, but the main watershed here did not come until 1872, with Martin Atock's appointment as locomotive superintendent; with the Ulster Railway the years 1864–5 saw the main foundation of locomotive practice being laid, as it lasted until 1880; on the Dublin & Drogheda Railway the significant shift from Sharp Stewart to Beyer Peacock occurred in 1863–4; on the system which from 1861 was controlled by the Belfast & Northern Counties Railway Company, the year 1856 saw the introduction of engines which continued in service until the 1920s; on the Dublin Wicklow & Wexford Railway the year 1864 saw the replacement of the old, outside-cylinder, Dublin & Kingstown locomotives by new, inside-cylinder engines and the introduction of standard main line types; finally, the year 1861 was of significance on the Waterford & Limerick Railway, with Atock's appointment and the scrapping of a number of the original engines.

From 1873 to 1960 the '101' or J15 class locomotives of the GS & WR were the most numerous class in the country. They were for over ninety years a standard engine, a sturdy 0–6–0 design used for all classes of traffic, including much passenger work at relatively high speeds. Introduced by Alexander McDonnell in 1866 from a design by Beyer Peacock of Manchester, the vast majority were built at Inchicore, the last batch in 1903. In all, 119 locomotives of this class ran on the GS & WR, two on the Dublin & Belfast Junction Railway, and while many of the older engines were scrapped in their original form, many were rebuilt in the 1930s with Belpaire superheated 'Z' type boilers and extended smokeboxes, and in 1947–8 fifteen of the class were temporarily converted to oil burning. But for dieselisation, the long story might have been even more remarkable and it is gratifying to know that two examples of this successful exercise in locomotive standardisation have been preserved.

Shown here is No 127, built at Inchicore in 1882.

A group of J15s at Inchicore running shed, about 1890.

On its formation by amalgamation in 1875–6 the GNR(I) acquired forty-one locomotives from one of its constituent companies, the Ulster Railway. Of these, nine had been built in the extensive Belfast shops, four of them being 0–4–2 goods engines with 5 ft driving wheels and cylinders measuring 16 in $\times$ 22 in, built between 1871 and 1876. **Tornado,** pictured here outside the Belfast running sheds in 1902, with Great Northern livery and numbering, was withdrawn in 1909.

An 0–4–2 goods locomotive of the Dublin Wicklow & Wexford Railway built in the Grand Canal Street works in 1889 to a Sharp Stewart design of 1864. Between 1864 and 1925 ten engines of this class were built and No 48, photographed here at Wexford, worked the main line goods until after the turn of the century.

This group of Great Northern locomotives photographed around the turn of the century at the old Belfast running sheds, just outside the present Great Victoria Street terminus, shows a number of engines of the period under consideration: No 114, **Lagan,** a 2–4–0 built at the Ulster Railway shops in Belfast in 1875–6; No 141, an 0–6–0 'AL' class locomotive, **Westmeath,** built by Beyer Peacock in 1894; No 146, **Wicklow,** an 0–6–0 of the 'A' class built by Beyer Peacock in 1888; No 89, a 4–2–2 passenger express engine supplied by Beyer Peacock in 1885.

This locomotive, **Albert,** and its companion **Victoria,** No 88, were the only bogie singles which ever ran in Ireland and with the exceptions of the old Sturrock engine, No 215, of the English 'Great Northern' and the two converted 'Great Western' broad-gauge engines, Nos 2001 and 2002, were the first of the type. The cylinders were 16 in × 22 in and the driving wheels 6 ft 7 in. For some years these two engines worked the 'Limited Mails' to and from Dublin, until superseded about 1892 by 4–4–0 engines. The two locomotives were withdrawn in 1904.

The Belfast & Northern Counties Railway Company, through its locomotive superintendent, Mr Bowman Malcolm, was noteworthy in its widespread use of compound engines and between 1890 and 1908, twenty-seven were constructed, in addition to two 0–6–0 goods engines. The most famous of all these was, perhaps, **Jubilee,** built as a 2–4–0 tender engine by Beyer Peacock in 1895, with 7 ft driving wheels, the largest ever in use in Ireland. The cylinders measured 18 in $\times$ 24 in and 18 in $\times$ 26 in and the original cost of the engine was £2,690. Both **Jubilee** and her sister locomotive **Parkmount,** while giving a good performance in traffic, were inclined to 'hunt' at top speed and as they were the fastest engines in Ireland on account of the large driving wheels, this was a considerable drawback. Accordingly, after a couple of years' service **Jubilee** was shopped and altered to a 4–4–0 type, with standard Beyer Peacock bogies. The experiment was successful and the engine gave excellent service in this form until 1926 when it was altered to a simple locomotive, with superheated boiler. **Jubilee** was withdrawn in 1946. This photograph shows No 50, as built.

Built at Broadstone in 1887, No 48, **Connaught,** a 'D' class 2–4–0 passenger express engine of the MGWR, was one of a notable sequence of locomotives of this type designed by the newly-appointed locomotive superintendent, Martin Atock, from 1873 onwards. The distinctive up-turned cab and bell-mouthed cast iron chimney were a feature of many Midland engines of the period. This particular locomotive was scrapped in 1920 but several of Atock's small 2–4–0s of the 1880s, rebuilt as 4–4–0s in 1900–1 with 5 ft 8 in driving wheels, survived into CIE days as the '530' class (D16). This photograph was taken at Broadstone in 1903.

One of the most attractive locomotives on one of the country's most picturesque lines, the 0–6–4 tanks of the Sligo Leitrim & Northern Counties Railway were built by Beyer Peacock, and fall into two groups— a smaller class introduced from 1882 to 1899, and a larger class from 1904 to 1951. **Hazlewood** was built in 1899 and remained in service until the line closed in the autumn of 1957. The locomotives of this company were identified solely by name.

This photograph shows Belfast & Northern Counties Railway Company's No 57 at Londonderry (Waterside) about 1902. A 'C' class 2–4–0 compound, built by Beyer Peacock in 1895 at a cost of £2450, this locomotive is of interest as being the first engine in the world to be fitted with a Ross 'Pop' safety valve, as shown. Ross was a Coleraine man and had the first experimental valve made in the York Road shops and fitted to No 57 shortly after delivery. The Ross safety valve, as developed, was for many years a standard fitting on British steam locomotives, and was also widely used overseas.

Two locomotives of the Cork Bandon & South Coast Railway, though falling marginally outside the boundaries of the period under review, can be considered here. Firstly, No 7, a 4–4–0 tank built at the Rocksavage shops in Cork in 1901, was the only locomotive built there in the long history of the company.

To the same company belongs the distinction of having owned and operated the only two American-built steam locomotives in the history of Irish railways. So busy were the principal locomotive builders in Britain in 1900 that, in that year, the Cork company ordered two 0–6–2 saddle tanks from Baldwin of Philadelphia. In keeping with the American locomotive tradition these had fairly short lives and were withdrawn around 1914. An interesting point to note is that, following many complaints, the American type whistles were removed a month or so after the engines arrived in Ireland.

THE ADVENT OF
NARROW-GAUGE RAILWAYS

The growing success of the broad-gauge railways in Ireland in the mid-nineteenth century led directly to the development of a remarkable extension of this 5 ft 3 in system on a much narrower gauge of 3 ft. This came as a direct result of the firm belief at Westminster that one of the chief means by which the lot of an area could be improved was to provide it with a railway. As many of the most impoverished areas in Ireland had neither the population nor the material resources to support a broad-gauge branch line, the idea was formulated of building 'feeder' lines on a 3 ft gauge, linking remote areas with main line stations and providing modest facilities for social and commercial intercourse. In some instances these lines were built solely with a view to serving the interests of a farming community; in others to provide facilities for the transport of minerals, rather as the 'tub boat' canals had done in an earlier age, but in most cases their lives were prolonged by seasonal excursion traffic through areas of great scenic beauty to coastal resorts largely created by the coming of the railway.

Today the light railways of Ireland are but a fond memory, one that lingers on long after the withdrawal of the numerous fascinating services which formerly traversed bleak turf bog and windswept moorland in the remoter corners of the most westerly country in Europe.

The first 3 ft gauge railway in Ireland opened in 1873. It was constructed by the Glenariff Iron Ore & Harbour Company high on the south-east side of the glen, and its purpose was to facilitate the export of iron ore from the new workings already begun in Cloughcor. The mines were a failure; the line lay idle from 1876, and in 1885 the locomotives and waggons were purchased by the Londonderry & Lough Swilly Railway Co. The line was left *in situ* in the vain hope that mining might start again at the head of the glen, and in June 1890 three miles of track were stolen overnight! This view shows the abandoned track, looking up Glenariff towards Parkmore and the mining area in Cloughcor.

The Ballymena Cushendall & Red Bay Railway was the first in Ireland to be authorised by Act of Parliament (July 1872). It had its origin in the iron ore workings around Cargan and Parkmore on the Antrim plateau, and as its name implies, the Act of 1872 envisaged a through route from Ballymena north-eastwards through the mining area and down to the coast at Red Bay by Glenballyemon, thus providing a line of export for the iron and bauxite workings through the small harbour at Waterfoot. This easterly portion of the initial proposal, beyond Retreat, was never built. The first section of the railway, from Bally-mena to Cargan, was opened for goods traffic in May 1875 and in the following year the rail head was advanced to Retreat! Numerous long sidings ran from the main line to the various ore workings in the Glenravel and Evishacrow districts, the ore being brought down to Ballymena and from there run through to Larne by the narrow-gauge Ballymena & Larne Railway, with which the Parkmore line was joined in 1880. In 1884 the BNCR Co acquired the Cushendall line and two years later introduced passenger traffic.

Shown here is the station at Parkmore in Midland Railway (Northern Counties Committee) days ie, after 1903, with ex-BC & RB Rly Co locomotive No 1, an 0–4–2 saddle tank built by Black, Hawthorn & Co of Gateshead in 1873–4, and a train consisting of a brake van with verandah ends (built 1898) and two earlier 'tramcar bogies', built by the BNCR.

The Ballymena & Larne Railway Company, incorporated in 1874, was authorised to construct a line from Harryville in Ballymena, to a junction with a line from Larne to Ballyclare, authorised in the previous year. The former proposal was in fact the result of determination on the part of the directors of the Larne & Ballyclare Railway Co to tap the iron ore deposits of Glenwhirry, and the Boards of the two companies showed a close similarity. The line from Larne to Ballyclare was opened in July 1877 and from Ballyboley Junction, on this line, to Harryville (Ballymena) for goods and passenger traffic in the following year.

Here (top) locomotive No 4 of the Ballymena & Larne Railway Co (a 2–4–0 side tank built by Beyer Peacock in 1878) heads a train consisting of a six-wheeled brake composite, two bogie brake composites and a first class saloon, clerestory roofed, leaving Larne Harbour in the 1880s. The lower photograph shows a coal train hauled by ex-Ballycastle Railway 4–4–2 tank No 113 storming up the Inver bank out of Larne, in the early days of the Second World War.

The Ballycastle Railway ran from the Belfast & Northern Counties station at Ballymoney through Dervock, Stranocum, Armoy and Capecastle, to Ballycastle, on the north Antrim coast. Opened in October 1880, like the two narrow-gauge lines serving Ballymena it passed subsequently to the control of the 'Northern Counties', later of the Midland Railway (Northern Counties Committee).

The upper photograph, taken at Ballycastle station early in the century, shows locomotive No 2, **Countess of Antrim,** a 'six-coupled' 0–6–0 saddle tank built in 1880 by Black, Hawthorn & Co of Gateshead, with a train consisting of two six-wheelers and a brake van. Below we see locomotive No 102 of the LMS (NCC), a 2–4–2 compound tank engine built in 1920 in Belfast (York Road) as No 112 by the Belfast & Northern Counties Railway Company, hauling a heavy holiday train out of Ballycastle across the Tow viaduct, 13 June 1936.

The Castlederg & Victoria Bridge Tramway was in fact a light railway running along the side of the public road between Victoria Bridge—a small station on the Great Northern line from Londonderry to Omagh and Enniskillen—and Castlederg, a prosperous market town $7\frac{1}{4}$ miles up the Derg valley, to the south-west. The line was opened in July 1884 and closed in January 1933. Shown here is a mixed train at Castlederg headed by a Hudswell Clark 0–4–4T, fitted with Stephenson valve gear, built in 1912 (C & VB No 5). The photograph was taken in August 1930.

The Clogher Valley Railway was constructed under an Order in Council dated 25 May 1884 under the Tramways Act (Ireland) of 1883. The line ran between Tynan and Maguiresbridge, both broad-gauge stations on the 'Great Northern' system, and provided a valuable service throughout an extensive agricultural area, serving such towns as Aughnacloy, Ballygawley, Clogher and Fivemiletown *en route*. The CVR opened in May 1887 and closed in December 1941. For most of its thirty-seven miles the railway ran along the side of the public road, though in places it 'took to the fields' and elsewhere ran down the centre of village streets.

The two photographs included here show, firstly, a flagman at Dempsey's Crossing, near Ballygawley, giving the right of way to a mixed special hauled by ex-Castlederg & Victoria Bridge locomotive No 4, rebuilt at Aughnacloy in 1936 as a 2–6–2 tank and, secondly, an Orangeman's Special to Caledon (12 July 1938) at Ballygawley. The two locomotives, here shown typically running backwards, are **Erne** and **Blackwater,** two 0–4–2 side tanks built by Sharp Stewart & Co in 1887. Note headlamp, cow-catcher and assorted rolling stock.

THE NARROW-GAUGE LINES OF COUNTY DONEGAL

The development of a widespread network of narrow-gauge lines in County Donegal, that remote, wind-swept corner of Ireland, is in itself a story of great engineering skill. The ingenious adaptation of a railway system to an inhospitable environment of great natural beauty, but with a minimum of resources, resulted in the emergence and successful operation, over the greater part of a century, of one of the largest narrow-gauge networks in Europe.

Because of the extent of the system, the nature of the terrain traversed and the volume of traffic forth-coming, the narrow-gauge railways of County Donegal were run with a fascinating assortment of steam locomotives and petrol and diesel railcars, which have already gained a place in the history of Irish railway working.

The Londonderry & Lough Swilly Railway system stemmed originally from an $8\frac{3}{4}$ mile line from Londonderry to Farland Point on Lough Swilly, subsequently replaced by Fahan as a point of steamboat arrival and departure. This initial section was on the 5 ft 3 in gauge and was opened in 1863. The line reached Buncrana the following year. In 1883 a line of railway was completed on the 3 ft gauge from Letterkenny to the L & LS Rly at Tooban Junction. It was another two years before the Buncrana-Londonderry line of the L & LS Rly was reduced in gauge, and the Letterkenny Railway was worked by the L & LS Rly Co from the outset. The extensions to Carndonagh and Burtonport, the latter a line traversing some of the most rugged and windswept country in Ireland, the former the most northerly in the country, were completed in 1901 and 1903 respectively.

Shown here is L & LS Rly Co's No 1, **J. T. Macky,** at Buncrana. This was an 0–6–2T originally built by Black, Hawthorn & Co of Gateshead in 1882 for the contractors on the Letterkenny line, McCrea & McFarland.

The Burtonport extension threaded its way out to the Atlantic seaboard across bleak moorland, sparsely populated, with poor thin soils and frequent outcrops of bare rock. The main engineering feature on the line was the Owencarrow viaduct, between Kilmacrennan and Creeslough. It was here on the evening of 30 January 1925 that a train was blown off the track, with the loss of four lives. An anemometer was subsequently installed at Dunfanaghy Road. Here we see (top) a 4–8–0 tender locomotive, with an 'up' mixed train, crossing the viaduct shortly after the line was opened, with below, a mixed train, again headed by a 4–8–0 tender locomotive, about to leave Burtonport, on the rugged Atlantic coast, June 1937. The Burtonport extension from Letterkenny closed on 3 June 1940.

The narrow-gauge railway system of the Donegal Railway Company (later the County Donegal Railways Joint Committee) was the largest network of its kind in the British Isles. Originating in a 5 ft 3 in gauge line up the Finn valley from Strabane to Stranorlar, the system grew steadily by amalgamation and extension until, at the time of its maximum extent, it had a total mileage of 124. West of Stranorlar the line led through the Barnesmore Gap to Donegal town, clinging to the side of a glacial trough, high above the valley bottom, and providing a rail journey unequalled in Ireland for scenic grandeur. The Killybegs branch line, with several stretches of exceedingly steep gradient (1 in 40) and charming views of Donegal Bay, carried the system out to the tattered fringe of maritime Europe.

The main administrative and operational centre of the system was Stranorlar, and here the 'down' evening 'Donegal Express' prepares to tackle the ascent into Barnesmore on a summer evening early in the century.

As the narrow-gauge system in County Donegal had reached its maximum extent, the necessity for dispensing with the watering of engines on the longer runs required a greater tank capacity and this was provided for in the three locomotives built by Nasmyth, Wilson & Co in 1912. As well as being the first narrow-gauge engines in the British Isles to be provided with superheaters, several other details of advanced locomotive design made them the most precocious narrow-gauge engines ever to run in Ireland. No 21, **Ballyshannon,** is seen here at Strabane shortly after delivery. This locomotive was renumbered 1, in 1928 and renamed **Alice** in the same year. A sister engine, **Strabane,** renamed **Blanche** in 1928, is now in the Transport Museum in Belfast. **Alice** was scrapped in 1961.

The last section of the extensive County Donegal narrow-gauge network to be built was the line from Strabane to Letterkenny, serving the towns of Convoy and Raphoe. This was constructed between 1904 and 1909 and was worked by the County Donegal Railways Joint Committee as a branch, from opening until the overall closure of the system on New Year's Day 1960.

Here we see work in progress on the Strabane & Letterkenny Railway: an erection team on the Foyle viaduct at Lifford (opposite top) with, below, one of Sir Robert McAlpine's contractor's engines at Ballindrait and, above, an 0–6–0 tank locomotive at the new station at Raphoe before the opening of the line on 1 January 1909.

The narrow-gauge railways of County Donegal were the scene of important pioneering work in the use of rail-cars and it was largely through the skill and foresight of the secretary and general manager, Henry Forbes, in introducing rail-car services, that the greater part of the far-flung network of 3 ft gauge track remained open until 1960.

This photograph, taken at Stranorlar in July 1931, shows the original petrol rail-car, though not in its original form, with a trailer car attached. Acquired from Allday & Onions of Birmingham in 1907 as an open inspection car, the vehicle was rebuilt in 1920, a Ford engine was fitted and the bodywork was enclosed to seat six persons. Forced into public service during the coal strike of 1926, between Glenties and Stranorlar, and Stranorlar and Strabane, it proved highly successful and it seems likely that, whereas as an inspection car it had been little used, as a rail-car it proved its worth and convinced Forbes of the important role which internal combustion rail vehicles could play on the Donegal system. Up to the end of April 1956 it had run over 19,000 miles; it was then withdrawn and is now in the Transport Museum in Belfast.

In 1931 the petrol rail-car fleet on the Donegal system, by now six in number, was augmented by the arrival of the first two diesel-engined vehicles. The underframes were built in the Great Northern shops at Dundalk, and the bodies by the Strabane firm of C. O'Doherty & Son. No 7, powered by a Gardner engine and with a remarkable wheel base, is shown here at Strabane soon after it went into service in June 1931. It was the first diesel-engined rail-car in the British Isles to operate regular time-table services.

NARROW-GAUGE RAILWAYS IN THE SOUTH AND WEST OF IRELAND

Of the steam-operated narrow-gauge railways in the south and west of Ireland, none now remains; but in their hey-day these lines provided a service to the community, both as suburban lines handling a heavy seasonal tourist traffic and as remote arteries of communication threading their way out to the Atlantic seaboard from main line stations on the major broad-gauge system to eastward.

Most of these lines were built under an Act of 1883 by which state assistance, in the shape of refunds of monies payable under 'Baronial Guarantee', was assured. Under the terms of this Act, the Treasury might repay to the barony one half of the amount which it might have paid under the guarantee, provided this did not exceed two per cent of the capital and that the line was open and carrying traffic. The guaranteeing area had to make good any deficit in working the line, but if the deficit continued over two years the railway became the property of the Grand Jury, operating through a Committee of Management, to be worked by them at their own expense. At the same time some relaxations were permitted from earlier Tramway Acts of 1860 and 1871 in the matter of speed, eg, where the distance of the line from the centre of the road was more than 30 ft, no speed restriction was enforced.

In the south and west the following narrow-gauge railways were built under the Act of 1883: the Schull & Skibbereen, the West & South Clare, the Cork & Muskerry and the Tralee & Dingle. Of these, all save the West & South Clare ran for part of their length along public highways, generally on a reserved track on one side.

The Cork Blackrock & Passage Railway was built originally on a 5 ft 3 in gauge (1847-50) but was extended and relaid on the 3 ft gauge between 1900 and 1904.

The Cavan & Leitrim Railway, a main line from Belturbet to Dromod, with a branch from Ballinamore to the coal and iron ore mining district around Arigna, was completed in 1888 and closed in April 1959. At Belturbet contact was made with the broad-gauge system of the GNR(I) and at Dromod with the Sligo branch of the Midland.

Here we see (opposite) locomotive No 7, **Olive,** a 4–4–0 side tank supplied by Robert Stephenson & Co in 1887 for the opening of the line, leaving Ballinamore with a mixed train in June 1932: (above) a general view of the interior of the Ballinamore locomotive shops, 1903; (below) locomotive No 4L, originally **Violet,** another of the eight tank engines with which the line opened in October 1887, brings a train of empty coal waggons from Dromod into Ballinamore in July 1955, on the C & L section of Coras Iompair Eireann. It is perhaps worth noting that the eight original locomotives were rebuilt early in the century and that No 2, **Kathleen,** is now preserved in the Transport Museum in Belfast.

The total length of the West Clare Railway was 53 miles, all single track. The section from Ennis to Miltown Malbay was built by the West Clare Railway Co between 1884 and 1887; that from Miltown Malbay to Kilkee and Kilrush by the South Clare Railways Co Ltd between 1884 and 1892. This latter was worked by the West Clare Railway Co from the outset. The system closed down in January 1961.

Immortalised by Percy French in 'Are ye right there Michael?' the West Clare system provided a route-way for the tourist wishing to savour the Atlantic breezes at Lahinch or Kilkee or visit the majestic cliffs of Moher.

Shown here (top) are locomotive No 3C, formerly **Ennistymon**, a 4–6–0 tank engine with outside bearings and Walschaerts valve gear, supplied by the Hunslet Engine Co of Leeds in 1922, one of the last two engines built for an Irish narrow-gauge line, with (below) locomotive No 11C on a summer excursion at Kilkee in July 1934. This engine was built by Bagnall of Stafford in 1909. Originally **Kilkee** of the West Clare Railway Co, it was withdrawn in 1953. Coaches on the West Clare were ballasted to withstand the high winds of the open Atlantic seaboard.

The Schull & Skibbereen Light Railway, $15\frac{1}{2}$ miles in length, was opened in September 1886 and was one of the least successful of all Irish narrow-gauge lines. It passed subsequently to the Grand Jury, later to the County Council, and as a line constructed under 'Baronial Guarantee' was throughout its existence a financial burden on the ratepayers of the area. Public services were withdrawn in 1946.

For the greater part of its length the railway ran along the side of the public road, linking the Cork Bandon & South Coast system at Skibbereen with the mining area of the Mizen Peninsula and the fishing port of Schull. The illustration here shows a mixed train at Hollyhill in July 1938, headed by locomotive No 4, formerly **Erin,** a 4–4–0 side tank built by Nasmyth, Wilson & Co in 1888 and in service until the line closed.

The Cork Blackrock & Passage Railway was built between 1847 and 1850 as a broad-gauge line from Cork down to the steam packet quay at Passage, a distance of some 6½ miles, single track. The line was extended to Crosshaven by Carrigaline between 1896 and 1904 on the 3 ft gauge and at the same time the 5 ft 3 in section, from Cork to Passage, was relaid on the narrow-gauge and the Cork-Blackrock section doubled. This latter section was the only instance in Ireland of a double-track, narrow-gauge railway.

Shown here is the re-opening of the bridge at Rochestown after it had been mined during the Civil War of 1922–3. All four locomotives of the narrow-gauge days of the CB & P Rly were 2–4–2 tanks built by Neilson, Reid & Co of Glasgow in 1899. They were noteworthy in having the largest driving wheels (4 ft 6 in) of any Irish narrow-gauge engines. The line closed in 1932 and the four locomotives were transferred to the Cavan & Leitrim Railway.

The Tralee & Dingle Light Railway was built under the Tramways (Ireland) Act of 1883 and completed in 1891. It linked Tralee, the main town in County Kerry, westwards across the spine of the Dingle peninsula by the Glenmore Pass and Glenagalt (680 ft asl), to Annascaul and Dingle. This main line was 31½ miles long and there was also a branch to Castlegregory, a further 6 miles. The ascent from Castlegregory Junction, where the branch line diverged, up to the summit at Glenagalt, was a steep climb of about four miles at more than 1 in 40. It was the most severe bank on any railway in Ireland and was the scene of a fatal derailment in 1893.

Livestock always played a prominent part in the traffic on this particular line and here a Fair train leaves Glenmore in July 1952 on the demanding journey across the Slieve Mish range to Castlegregory Junction. The locomotive is No 2T, a 2–6–0T built by the Hunslet Engine Co of Leeds in 1889 and supplied originally to the contractor building the line. It was noteworthy as a six-coupled narrow-gauge engine with Walschaerts valve gear. It was rebuilt in 1902 and remained in service until the line closed.

Passenger services were withdrawn in April 1939 and regular daily goods services in 1947. Thereafter, until June 1953, the only traffic on the line was a once-monthly service of Fair Specials, as shown, run down light to Dingle on the last Friday of each month for the livestock fair on the following day, and returning to Tralee that evening. The lightness of the train here is accounted for by the fact that it was the second Fair Special on that particular weekend.

The Cork & Muskerry Light Railway had a total length of 26½ miles. The original line was from Cork to Blarney (opened 1887) with a branch to Coachford, completed in March of the following year. The main incentive in building the railway was the tourist traffic to Blarney. Between 1890 and 1893 the system was completed with the construction of the 8½ mile Donoughmore Extension Railway, worked by the Cork & Muskerry from the outset. The railway was never very successful, depending entirely on 'Baronial Guarantee' for continued existence. Services were withdrawn at the end of 1934.

The illustration above shows the largest locomotive the Cork & Muskerry possessed, a 4–4–0 outside cylinder tank, with inside bearings to the coupled wheels, outside to the bogies. Built by the Brush Electrical Engineering Co in 1897, this engine carried the name **Peake** and was No 7 in the system, becoming No 7K with the amalgamation under the GSR in 1925, and broken up in 1935. It is shown here at the engine shed at Donoughmore.

The line constructed between Listowel and Ballybunion in County Kerry was unique in the British Isles. It was constructed on a principle devised by a Frenchman, Lartigue, and quite simply was an early form of monorail. A single elevated rail was carried on angle iron trestles about 3 ft 6 in high, with a light guide rail on each side, about 2 ft below the carrying rail, the whole supported on steel plates resting on steel sleepers. The system was supposed to be particularly suitable for lines being built in rough or undeveloped country and this no doubt explains the selection of this remote area of County Kerry, on the Shannon estuary, as a suitable location for the first venture, outside France, by the Lartigue Railway Construction Co. The line was $9\frac{1}{4}$ miles in length and linked Listowel, a market town on the Limerick-Tralee section of the Waterford & Limerick Railway, with Ballybunion, a small seaside resort on the Shannon estuary. The line was opened on 29 February 1888 and with initial success it was hoped that the Lartigue system might be used elsewhere in the construction of Irish light railways.

This panorama of the Lartigue lay-out at Ballybunion about the turn of the century shows a turntable (foreground) used in making up the trains or in shunting, sections of the monorail itself, a locomotive and various items of rolling stock.

A more detailed view of one of the three tender locomotives supplied by Hunslet of Leeds for the opening of the Listowel & Ballybunion Railway in 1888, which worked the system until it closed down in October 1924. These had twin horizontal boilers on either side of the central rail, each having a separate firebox and cab. Each boiler provided steam for four cylinders, two on the engine itself and two on the tender. Each locomotive weighed $4\frac{1}{4}$ tons and was equipped with a more than adequate headlamp.

STEAM TRAMWAYS AND HORSE TRACTION

In several parts of Ireland the roadside steam tramway was a distinctive feature of the landscape. In Irish railway history it is extremely difficult to say exactly where a steam tramway ends and a light railway begins, and for practical purposes I have in this allowed myself to be guided by the nature of the picture selected to illustrate each system. If the subject of the photograph is to all intents and purposes a narrow-gauge railway train, albeit running along the side of a public road, I have been inclined to include it in the section dealing with Irish narrow-gauge lines. If, on the other hand, the photograph quite clearly depicted a 'tram' driven by a steam locomotive of the tramway type, then I considered it for inclusion here.

Constructed mainly in suburban areas, or linking outlying villages with the transport systems of urban authorities, these steam tramways have long since disappeared, replaced in some cases by electrified lines, in others stifled by the advent of road transport.

Yet another pleasant feature of the Irish rail transport scene which has disappeared was the use formerly made of basic 'horse power' on certain branch lines, north and south.

From 1877 to 1915 a horse tramway linked the Great Northern rail head at Warrenpoint, County Down, with the quiet little resort of Rostrevor, some three miles away along the shore of Carlingford Lough. Here two of the single-deck, four-wheeler trams, each seating twenty-four passengers, are seen at the Rostrevor terminus, opposite the railway company's hotel. The horse-drawn service was run in connection with train arrivals and departures at Warrenpoint.

The famous horse tram at Fintona, County Tyrone, ran from 1854 to 1957, linking Fintona Junction on the Omagh-Enniskillen branch of the Great Northern system, with the little town of Fintona, a distance of just over half a mile. The original Fintona tramcar, in use from 1854 to 1883, was replaced in that year by the well known 'double decker' built by the Metropolitan Co at a cost of £205. First and second class passengers were carried in the lower saloon, under cover and separated by a partition. Access was from the terminal platforms through sliding doors. Narrow spiral stairs led to the open upper deck (third class) which had a longitudinal back-to-back seat running the full length of the deck. The tram is seen here at Fintona in October 1926 just outside the station accommodation. The open truck is being taken up to the Junction to act as a 'buffer' between a normal closed van and the tram itself, on the return journey. Otherwise the body of the van coming in contact with the staircase of the tram prevented effective coupling. The tram itself is now in the Transport Museum in Belfast.

At Upperlands, County Londonderry, a private branch line ran from the station on the Derry Central main line up to the linen bleach green and power loom weaving factory of William Clark & Son. Inside the works boundary this branch, on the normal 5 ft 3 in gauge, had various offshoots and, in addition, connected up with several short stretches of line, laid down on the 2 ft gauge. It was these narrow-gauge lines which were horse-worked. A horse drew open 'floats', long and narrow and with terminal bogies, from the 'Green' itself up to the main office block and dispatch area where the linen was finally checked and 'entered' before being returned to the broad-gauge branch line for dispatch to Belfast and overseas. The photograph reproduced here was taken in 1958.

The first roadside steam tramway in Ireland, the Portstewart Tramway in north Londonderry, opened in June 1882. It linked the seaside resort with its railway station, some two miles distant, and trams ran in connection with the principal train services. The private company operating the line at the outset failed and in 1887 the tramway passed to the Belfast & Northern Counties Railway Company, subsequently to the Midland Railway (Northern Counties Committee) and lastly, from 1923, to the LMS (NCC). The tramway closed down in January 1926.

Shown here in September 1925, is a mixed tram at Victoria Terrace (Atlantic Circle), where there was a passing loop. The locomotive, No 3, was supplied by Kitson & Co of Leeds in 1900, an 0–4–0T believed to have been the last tramway-type engine built by that firm. The other two engines of the tramway are in Transport Museums: No 1 in Hull, No 2 in Belfast.

The Cavehill & Whitewell Tramway opened just over a year after the Portstewart Tramway. It ran along the side of the Antrim Road in Belfast, from Chichester Park to Glengormley. The company possessed three 0–4–0 tramway engines by Kitson of Leeds, and on the double-decker trailers, first class passengers travelled inside, second class on top. This photograph shows locomotive No 1, with which the line was opened in 1882, at Chichester Park around 1890. To the rear can be seen a four-wheeled, double-deck horse tram of the Belfast Corporation Tramways, a service linking up with the steam tramway and conveying passengers to and from the Castle Junction.

The Dublin & Blessington Steam Tramway, completed in 1888, ran from Terenure south-westwards by Templeogue and Tallaght to Blessington, subsequently to Poulaphouca, an overall distance of some 20 miles. The Blessington-Poulaphouca extension was constructed by a separate company but the 'Dublin & Blessington' enjoyed running powers over the line and supplied the rolling stock. At Terenure, contact was made with the terminus of the Dublin United Tramways and, unlike the Lucan line, the Blessington track was laid on a 5 ft 3 in gauge, with a view to facilitating through working. The Poulaphouca extension closed down in 1927, the Blessington-Terenure line in 1932.

Shown here outside the Templeogue depot is locomotive No 3, an 0–4–0 well tank locomotive, with added saddle tank, built in 1887 by the Falcon Works, Loughborough, at a cost of £900, and scrapped in 1927; a composite double-decker trailer car of the standard steam tram type, seating 68 passengers, and a covered goods waggon, both also built by the Falcon Works in Loughborough.

Completed in 1883, the line of the Dublin & Lucan Steam Tramway ran from the terminus of the Dublin United Tramways at Conyngham Road, out to the village of Lucan, a distance of about 7 miles. An extension was built subsequently from Lucan to Leixlip, a distance of just under 2 miles, by a separate company, but this extension was worked by the original company. The line ran along a slightly raised track on the side of the public road, and it was electrified at the end of the century. Our photograph, taken in 1895, shows two school excursions at Ballydowd, about a mile east of Lucan. The locomotive in the foreground, No 6, a standard tramway 0–4–0 tank engine, was built by Kitson of Leeds in 1887.

HYDRO-ELECTRIC TRAMWAYS

Two of the most interesting developments in the history of Irish railways were not railways in the generally accepted sense, but roadside tramways operated by hydro-electricity. These ran between Portrush and the Giant's Causeway in north Antrim, a distance of about 8 miles, and between the mill village of Bessbrook, in south Armagh, and the town and port of Newry, some 3 miles distant.

The County Antrim system opened in January 1883 and while electric traction was not introduced until a few months later this was undoubtedly the first hydro-electric road 'rail-way' in the world. The route of the Giant's Causeway, Portrush & Bush Valley Railway & Tramway Company's line lay between the BNCR station in Portrush and the town of Bushmills, whence jaunting cars and horse charabancs ran up to the Causeway Hotel at the entrance to the Causeway itself. The line was laid along the seaward side of the public road, overlooking the Atlantic, and current was taken from a side conductor rail carried some 17 in from the ground on wooden posts and 22 in from the inside rail of the tramway itself. To operate the line in Portrush, two steam tramway locomotives were ordered from Wilkinson & Co of Wigan and it was with one of these that services began early in 1883.

A power station was constructed on the river Bush, with two Alcott water turbines developing 90 hp, and at the Portrush depot a 25 hp stationary steam engine drove a dynamo generating 250 volts. Regular electric services were introduced later in 1883. The line was subsequently extended to a point close to the Causeway entrance, and over the years a wide assortment of electric cars and trailers saw service on a line which soon became something of a national institution. Supply of current by overhead wire and trolley was introduced in 1899 but many of the early cars and trailers remained in use, suitably adapted, until the tramway closed down in September 1949.

The Bessbrook and Newry Tramway opened in October 1885 and unlike its counterpart in north Antrim, which was designed solely to convey a heavy seasonal passenger traffic to and from a world-famous tourist attraction, the Bessbrook line served as a link between the picturesque mill village, a Quaker foundation planned and built as a model community earlier in the century, and the historic town and port of Newry. It was the intention of the Bessbrook & Newry Tramway Company that, in addition to passenger services, a regular traffic in a variety of merchandise—fuel, raw materials and finished goods—should pass up and down the line. To this end, a fleet of flangeless waggons designed by Mr Henry Barcroft, a director of the Bessbrook Spinning Co and a talented mechanical engineer, was introduced on the tramway from the outset. These could run on either road or rail and, when on the tramway itself, they ran on smaller rails laid just outside the main track and at a slightly lower level. In its prosperous days the Bessbrook tramway carried annually an average of 16,000 tons of goods and merchandise. A Newry the tramway terminated in the Edward Street station of the Great Northern; at Bessbrook, in the yard of the great flax spinning mill. The line closed down in January 1948.

This view of around 1895 shows the Causeway tram at Dunluce Castle, travelling towards Bushmills. Motive power is provided by one of Wilkinson's steam locomotives (No 2, delivered at the beginning of 1883) with Trailer Cars No 10, a five bench open toast-rack, and No 1, an enclosed saloon with covered platforms at each end and clerestory roof.

At the Causeway terminus, about 1895, we see Motor Car No 4 and, again, Trailer Car No 10 (note here the 'third rail', the decorative side panel and the oriental shelter kiosk).

This artist's impression of the hydro-electric power station at Walkmills on the river Bush, a short distance above Bushmills, shows the two original Alcott turbines which were replaced by larger turbines from Turnbull of Edinburgh in 1901 and 1903. The original power station lay-out contained many features of considerable interest in the history of electrical technology.

Motor Car No 20 of the Causeway tramway, a new toast-rack type obtained for the inauguration of the overhead system in 1899. It is seen here with two trailers, at the White Rocks near Portrush, in August 1947, shortly before the tramway closed down.

No 4 Motor Car of the Bessbrook & Newry Tramway, supplied by Messrs Hurst, Nelson & Co of Motherwell in 1921, crosses the public road at the Millvale crossing, near Bessbrook. The car was divided into two compartments, with a sliding door between. Longitudinal seats along each side accommodated thirty-two passengers and there was a luggage compartment at the driving end, marked by a roll-up door. At the Millvale crossing the central rail which formed the conductor over the rest of the line was replaced by an overhead wire, tapped by bow collectors on the roofs of the cars. This photograph, taken immediately after the Second World War, also shows a trailer car of the former Dublin & Lucan Tramway and, to the right, the flour mill on the Camlough river in which the original MacAdam water turbine, built on Thomson's inward flow, vortex design of 1850, was installed in 1885, driving directly to two Edison-Hopkinson dynamos. A horse power of 62 was translated into an average current of 72 amps at 1000 rpm.

ACCIDENTS

Accidents on Irish railways fall into two classes, those which were purely accidental and those which were contrived. Of the former, by far the most serious was the Armagh disaster of June 1889, followed by the Ballymacarrett collision of January 1945. Not all accidents were accompanied by loss of life and, in retrospect, the amusing side of many of them can be appreciated, as for instance when one of Adams' light engines of the Londonderry & Enniskillen Railway was derailed by a cow near Porthall and ran for a short distance, cutting furrows in the ground until it became firmly stuck in soft earth; or when a train and steam roller collided on the Cork & Muskerry Light Railway.

The accidents resulting from terrorist activity fall into two main periods, the Civil War of 1922–3, which followed the declaration of an Irish Republic, and a much less widespread campaign of minor derailments and explosions in Ulster in the mid 1950s, part of a campaign directed by the Irish Republican Army against the Government of Northern Ireland.

Early in the morning of 8 February 1864, the 2.30 Mallow-Killarney 'night goods', consisting of fifteen waggons and two brake vans, was maliciously diverted onto a private siding running to Webb's Mills at Quartertown, about one mile from Mallow. On this siding the train came up against some empty waggons and pushing these on ahead of it soon came to a violent stop against the wall of a corn store. Why the engine driver did not notice long before the impact occurred that his train had been switched onto a private siding, or how the guard (the only other person on the train) came to be seriously injured, is not clear from contemporary press reports, but the illustration here is of considerable interest as being in all probability the earliest surviving pictorial record of an Irish railway accident, or indeed of a steam locomotive on Irish soil.

The derailment of a southbound passenger express at Brackagh Moss, $2\frac{1}{2}$ miles south of Portadown, on the Great Northern main line, was believed to have been caused by defective permanent way. This accident occurred on 30 June 1886 and resulted in the loss of six lives, with twenty-nine injured.

The tragic story of the Armagh disaster of 12 June 1889 is well known. The bare facts are that on a sustained climb on the hilly Armagh-Markethill-Newry line, close to Hamiltonsbawn, a heavy excursion train out from Armagh, bound for Warrenpoint, ran out of steam. In an attempt to resolve a difficult situation, the train was divided by the crew, whereupon the ten rearmost carriages, heavily crowded with Sunday School children, ran backwards towards Armagh and on a high embankment just outside the city, collided violently with a regular passenger train from Armagh to Newry. Eighty people died and 260 were injured in an accident which prompted immediate parliamentary legislation, making compulsory the use of the automatic vacuum brake and block telegraph system on all public railways.

The engine of the regular passenger train from Armagh to Newry, which bore the full force of the impact, was thrown from the rails but was surprisingly little damaged. It was an 0–4–2, belonging originally to the Dublin & Drogheda Railway Company and built by Beyer Peacock at Gorton in 1858. Here we see a remarkable close-up view of the derailed engine, accurate in detail, which appeared in the *Illustrated London News* of 22 June 1889, a wood-cut based on an original photograph by Messrs Hunter & Co of Armagh.

On 14 February 1900 a most remarkable accident occurred in the Harcourt Street terminus of the Dublin Wicklow & Wexford Railway Company, when a heavy cattle train from Enniscorthy failed to stop, ploughed through a 3 ft thick wall and came to rest with the locomotive on top of the buffer stops which had fallen into Hatch Street, a busy Dublin thoroughfare, some 24 ft below. Miraculously, no one was killed.

On the County Donegal narrow-gauge system, the evening train of Sunday 7 September 1913 from Londonderry (Victoria Road) to Strabane approached Donemana station at a speed estimated at around 40 mph, despite the fact that a speed limit of 6 mph was in force at the passing loop there. The locomotive, No 19 **Letterkenny,** and the first two carriages, left the rails and heeled over. One person was killed, another seriously injured, and the driver of the train was found later to have left Derry in a state of intoxication.

The Civil War of 1922–3, between the Irish Free State and the Irish Republican Army, was a time of vicious guerilla attacks on Irish railways, particularly in the south-east of the country, in Counties Wexford and Waterford. Two incidents have been chosen to illustrate the nature of the terrorist activity. At the Wexford end of the Killurin tunnel (above), alongside the Slaney, two lengths of rail were removed on the night of 15 August 1922 and the 'down' Night Mail, a goods train with 22 waggons, principally of coal, was derailed and ran for 167 yards on the sleepers until the locomotive reached softer ground, and heeled over. The line was re-opened within thirty-six hours.

In August 1922 one of the arches of the viaduct at Ballyvoile, on the Waterford-Mallow line, was blown up in an incident in the Civil War, and later several other arches gave way. The line from Waterford out as far as Durrow, on the east side of the viaduct, was the scene of several derailments at about the same time, and in the early hours of 31 January 1923 a ballast train, which had been engaged on repair work, left the area for Waterford. It was intercepted and sent back westwards towards the viaduct, ending its journey in a spectacular fashion with locomotive No 189, an Inchicore J15, at the foot of the viaduct piers and the ballast train itself draped crazily over the truncated approach embankment.

On 30 January 1925 the rearmost portion of a narrow-gauge train consisting of a 4–6–2 tank engine, a covered waggon and three carriages, was blown off the Owencarrow viaduct on the Burtonport extension of the Londonderry & Lough Swilly system in County Donegal. Four persons were killed and another four seriously injured.

On 6 September 1927 a curious accident occurred on the Cork & Muskerry Light Railway when the 7.45 am passenger train from Donoughmore was approaching Cork. About a mile on the Cork side of Carrigrohane station and about 4 miles from Cork, the train collided violently with a steam roller engaged on road repairs, and considerable damage was caused. Ambulances rushed to the scene but, apart from a few ladies who fainted, no one was injured. The following day's newspapers described how the impact occurred:

> . . . the driver of the train claimed that he blew his whistle when within 40 yards of the steam roller, and again when he was near it, but on the other hand the driver of the steam roller claims that he signalled to the driver of the train to stop and his signal was not responded to . . .

Local wags held that the steam roller was racing the train!

INDEX

SOURCES AND ACKNOWLEDGMENTS

The author is grateful to the following for permission to reproduce illustrations: William Robb, 45, 48 (bottom), 52 (top), 69 (bottom), 70 (bottom); H. C. Casserley, 46 (bottom), 65 (top), 71, 75 (bottom), 82, 84 (bottom), 85; Walter McGrath, 47 (both pictures), 53 (bottom), 86, 88, 93, 108 (bottom); Dr E. M. Patterson, 48 (top), 52 (bottom); Leslie Hyland, 54; W. A. Camwell, 55; P. J. Currivan, 60; Dr G. Gillespie, 72, 73; Mrs N. McCarter, 68; L. G. Marshall, 83 (bottom); Maurice Batley, 92; Hallam Ashley, 100; D. G. Coakham, 101; Raymond McGrath, 25 (both figures); R. N. Clements, 23 (bottom), 27 (bottom), 36 (bottom), 46 (top), 66 (bottom), 84 (top), 87; J. H. Houston, 17, 18, 21 (top), 63, 69 (top); J. E. Kite, 22 (centre); G. R. Mahon, 33 (top); Duffner Bros, Dundalk, 45 (inset); Public Record Office Ireland, 10; Office of Public Works Dublin, 9; Public Record Office Northern Ireland, 8, 33 (bottom), 76, 77, 78 (both pictures), 79, 81, 106 (top); National Library of Ireland, 12 (both pictures), 26, 27 (top), 30, 31 (bottom), 32 (top), 35 (both pictures), 37, 41 (top), 49 (bottom), 51, 57 (both pictures), 67, 75 (top), 89, 90, 95 (top), 98 (top); Ministry of Finance Northern Ireland, 28 (top), 32 (bottom), 34 (bottom), 36 (top), 38, 41 (bottom); Ian Allan Ltd, 13 (top), 14 (top), 20, 23 (top), 49 (top), 62, 66 (top); Science Museum, London, 13 (bottom), 95 (bottom); CIE, 22 (top); Irish Railway Record Society, 22 (bottom), 59, 61 (both pictures), 64, 65 (bottom), 83 (top), 105 (bottom), 106 (bottom), 107 (both pictures); Ulster Journal of Archaeology, 28 (bottom), 39 (both figures); Ulster Folk Museum 34 (top), 43 (top), 70 (top); Green Studio Ltd, Dublin, 42 (top left); Ulster Museum, 42 (top right), 43 (bottom), 44, 50, 98 (bottom); Allison Studio, Armagh, 56 (top); Armagh County Museum, 56 (bottom), 91; Locomotive & General Railway Photographs, 74; Real Photographs Co Ltd, Southport, 80; Linenhall Library, Belfast, 94, 108 (top); Thos H. Mason & Sons (Ltd), Dublin, 96; Belfast Telegraph, 103; Electrical Times, 99.

A full list of acknowledgments and sources, and a comprehensive bibliography, will appear at the end of the second volume but the author felt that an opportunity could not go by at this stage without acknowledging a particular debt of gratitude to Mr R. N. Clements of Celbridge, County Kildare, whose general advice and guidance throughout the entire project have been invaluable.